100 Christmas Carols

FOR UKULELE

ISBN 978-1-4950-2567-9

HAL•LEONARD® CORPORATION

7777 W. BLUEMOUND RD. P.O. BOX 13819 MILWAUKEE, WI 53213

In Australia Contact:
Hal Leonard Australia Pty. Ltd.
4 Lentara Court
Cheltenham, Victoria, 3192 Australia
Email: ausadmin@halleonard.com.au

Visit Hal Leonard Online at
www.halleonard.com

CONTENTS

Angels from Heaven

Traditional Hungarian

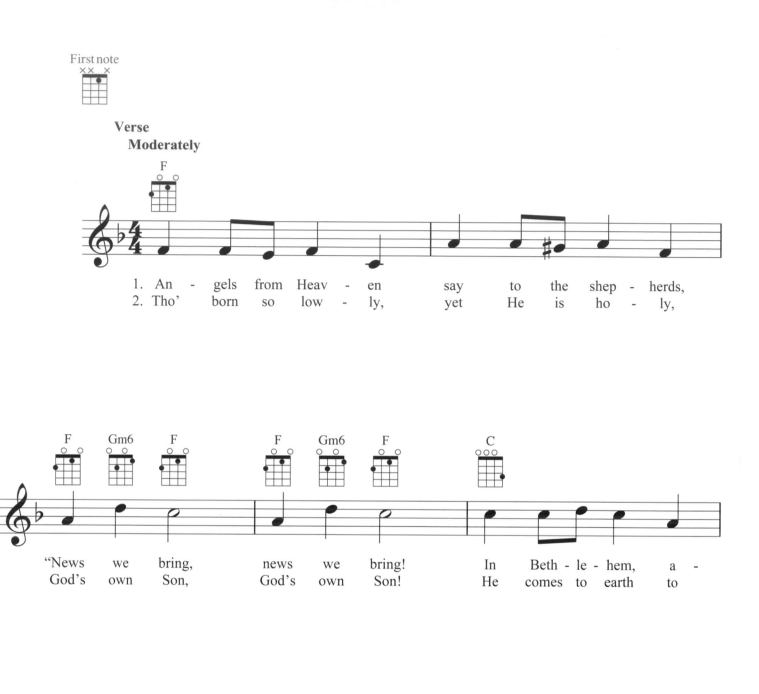

1. An - gels from Heav - en say to the shep - herds,
2. Tho' born so low - ly, yet He is ho - ly,

"News we bring, news we bring! In Beth - le - hem, a -
God's own Son, God's own Son! He comes to earth to

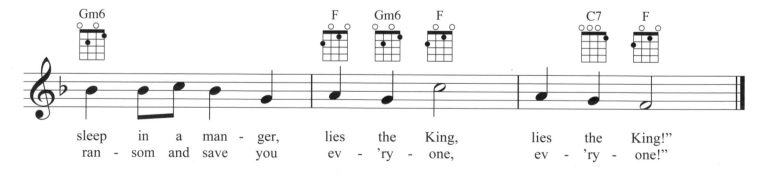

sleep in a man - ger, lies the King, lies the King!"
ran - som and save you ev - 'ry - one, ev - 'ry - one!"

Angels from the Realms of Glory

Words by James Montgomery
Music by Henry T. Smart

Angels We Have Heard on High

Traditional French Carol
Translated by James Chadwick

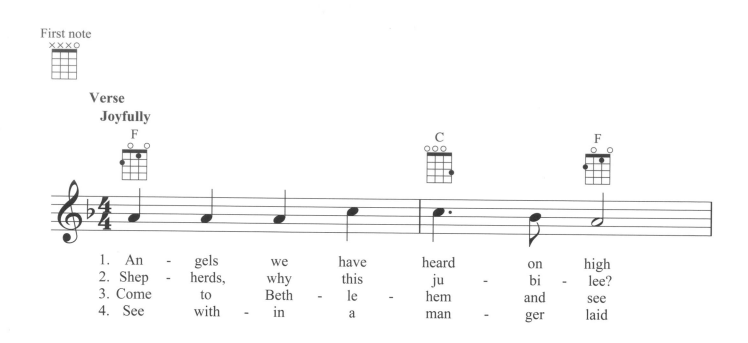

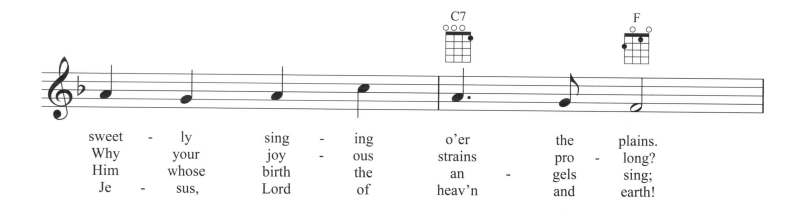

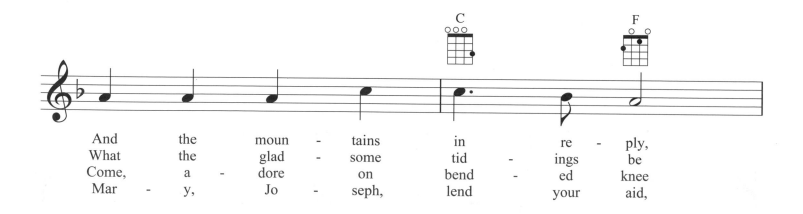

ech - o - ing their joy - ous strains.
which in - spire your heav - 'nly song?
Christ the Lord, the new - born King.
with us sing our Sav - ior's birth.

Chorus

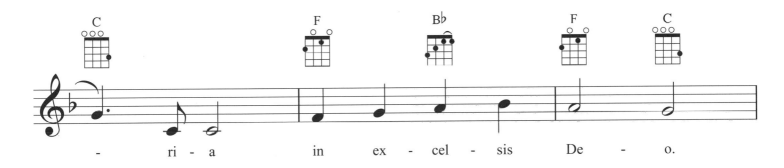

Glo - -

- ri - a in ex - cel - sis De - o.

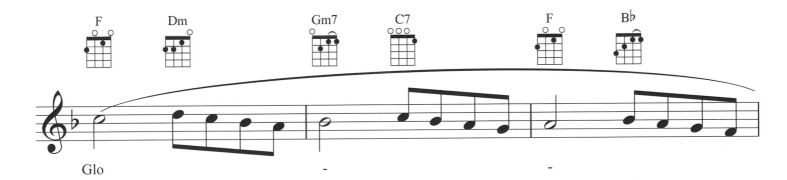

Glo - -

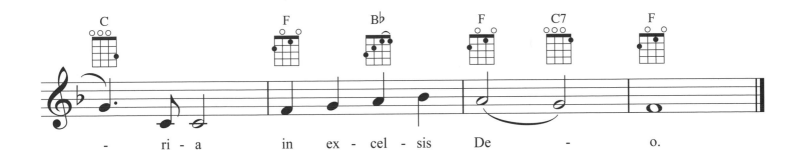

- ri - a in ex - cel - sis De - o.

As Each Happy Christmas

Traditional

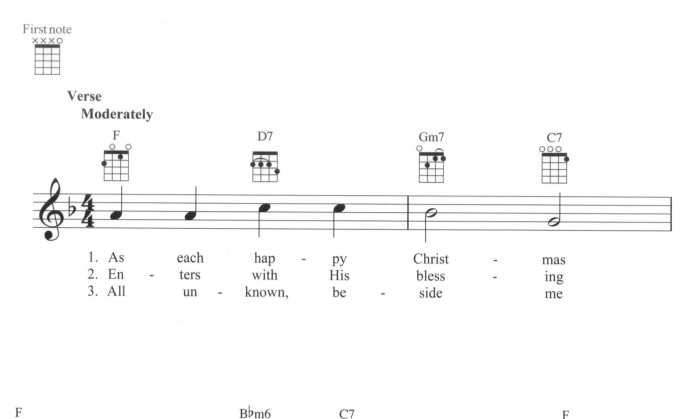

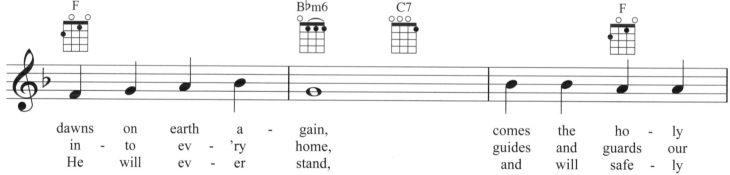

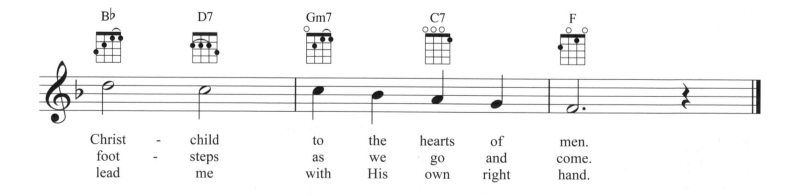

1. As each hap - py Christ - mas
2. En - ters with His bless - ing
3. All un - known, be - side me

dawns on earth a - gain, comes the ho - ly
in - to ev - 'ry home, guides and guards our
He will ev - er stand, and will safe - ly

Christ - child to the hearts of men.
foot - steps as we go and come.
lead me with His own right hand.

As Lately We Watched

19th Century Austrian Carol

First note

Verse
Brightly

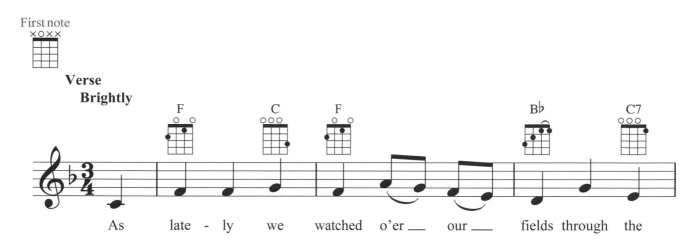

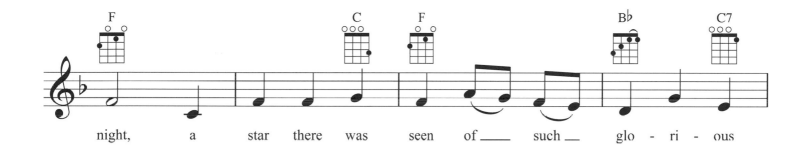

As late-ly we watched o'er __ our __ fields through the

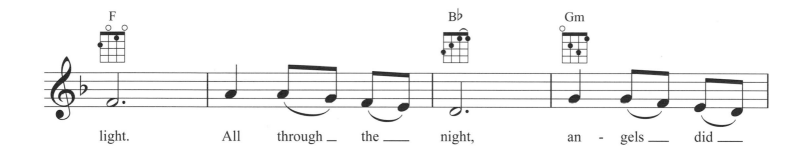

night, a star there was seen of __ such __ glo-ri-ous

light. All through __ the __ night, an-gels __ did __

sing in car-ols so sweet of __ the __ birth of the King.

As with Gladness Men of Old

Words by William Chatterton Dix
Music by Conrad Kocher

Away in a Manger

Traditional
Words by John T. McFarland (v.3)
Music by William J. Kirkpatrick

Away in a Manger

Words by John T. McFarland (v. 3)
Music by James R. Murray

Beside Thy Cradle Here I Stand

from THE CHRISTMAS ORATORIO
Words by Paul Gerhardt
Translated by Rev. J. Troutbeck
Music from the *Geistliche Gesangbuch*

Verse
Slowly, with feeling

Be - side ___ Thy cra - dle here I stand, O ___

Thou that ev - er ___ liv - est, and bring ___ Thee with a

will - ing hand the ___ ver - y gifts Thou ___ giv - est. Ac -

cept me; 'tis my mind ___ and heart, my soul, my strength, my

ev - 'ry part that ___ Thou from me de - sir - est.

A Baby in the Cradle

By D.G. Corner

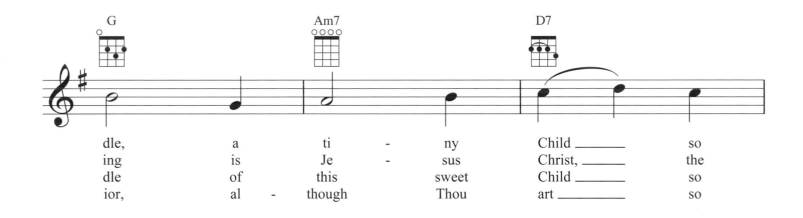

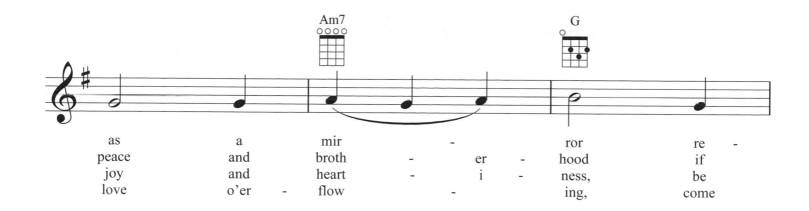

as   a   mir -   ror   re -
peace   and   broth -   er - hood   if
joy   and   heart -   i - ness, be
love o'er - flow - ing, come

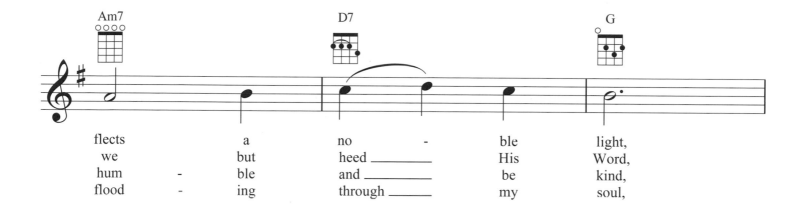

flects   a   no - ble light,
we   but   heed ____ His Word,
hum - ble and ____ be kind,
flood - ing through ____ my soul,

this   ti - ny Child ____ so
doth Je - sus Christ, ____ the
for Mar - y's Child ____ so
Thou love - ly Babe ____ so

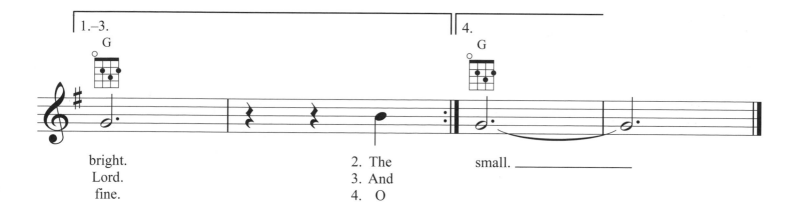

bright.
Lord.
fine.

2. The   small. ____
3. And
4. O

15

Bells Over Bethlehem

Traditional Andalusian Carol

The Boar's Head Carol

Traditional English Carol

1. The boar's head in hand bear I, be-decked with bays and
2. The boar's head, as I un-der-stand, is the rar-est dish in
3. Our stew-ard hath pro-vid-ed this in hon-or of the

rose - mar - y. And I pray you, my mas - ters, be mer - ry, quot
all this land, which thus be - decked with a gay gar - land, let
King of bliss, which on this day to be serv - ed is, in

es - tis in con - vi - vi - o.
us ser - vi - re can - ti - co.
Re - gi - nen - si a - tri - o.

Ca - put a - pri

de - fe - ro, red - dens lau - des Do - mi - no.

A Boy Is Born in Bethlehem

Traditional

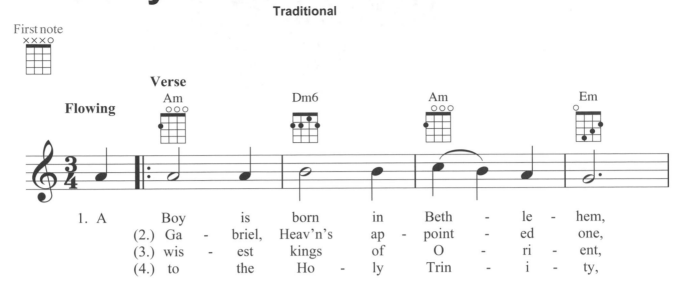

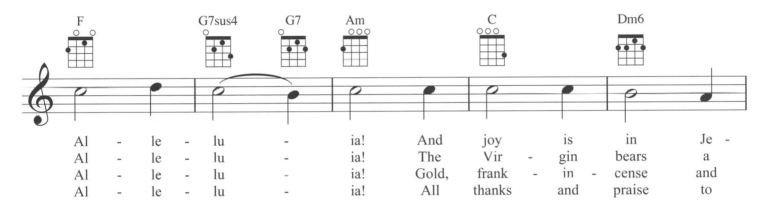

1. A Boy is born in Beth - le - hem,
(2.) Ga - briel, Heav'n's ap - point - ed one,
(3.) wis - est kings of O - ri - ent,
(4.) to the Ho - ly Trin - i - ty,

Al - le - lu - ia! And joy is in Je - a -
Al - le - lu - ia! The Vir - gin bears a
Al - le - lu - ia! Gold, frank - in - cense and
Al - le - lu - ia! All thanks and praise to

ru - sa - lem. Al - le - lu - ia, Al - le -
ho - ly Son. Al - le - lu - ia, Al - le -
myrrh pre - sent. Al - le - lu - ia, Al - le -
God Most High. Al - le - lu - ia, Al - le -

- lu - ia!   2. Through
- lu - ia!   3. The
- lu - ia!   4. Laud
- lu -   ia!

Break Forth, O Beauteous, Heavenly Light

from THE CHRISTMAS ORATORIO
Words by Johann Rist
Translated by Rev. J. Troutbeck
Melody by Johann Schop
Arranged by J.S. Bach

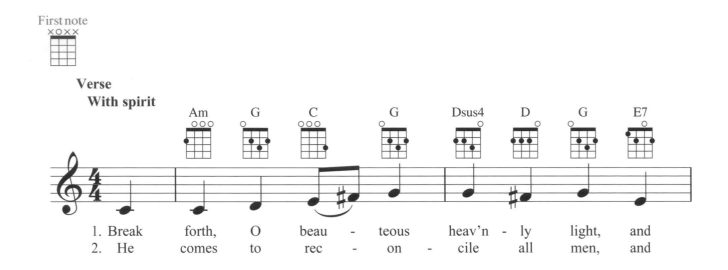

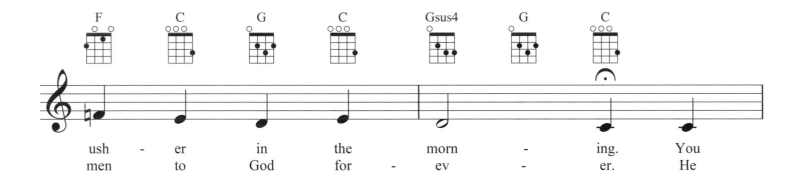

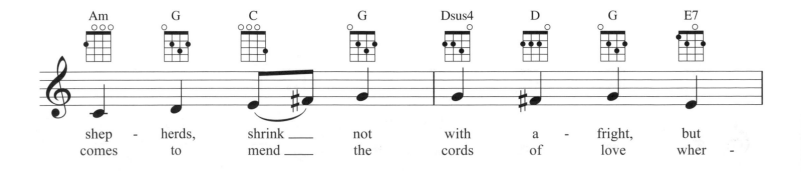

1. Break forth, O beau - teous heav'n - ly light, and
2. He comes to rec - on - cile all men, and

ush - er in the morn - ing. You
men to God for - ev - er. He

shep - herds, shrink not with a - fright, but
comes to mend not the cords of love wher -

Bring a Torch, Jeannette, Isabella

17th Century French Provençal Carol

First note

Verse
Brightly

1. Bring a torch, ___ Jean - nette, Is - a -
2. *See additional lyrics*

bel - la; bring a torch, ___ come swift - ly and

run. Christ is born, tell the folk of the

vil - lage, Je - sus is sleep - ing in His

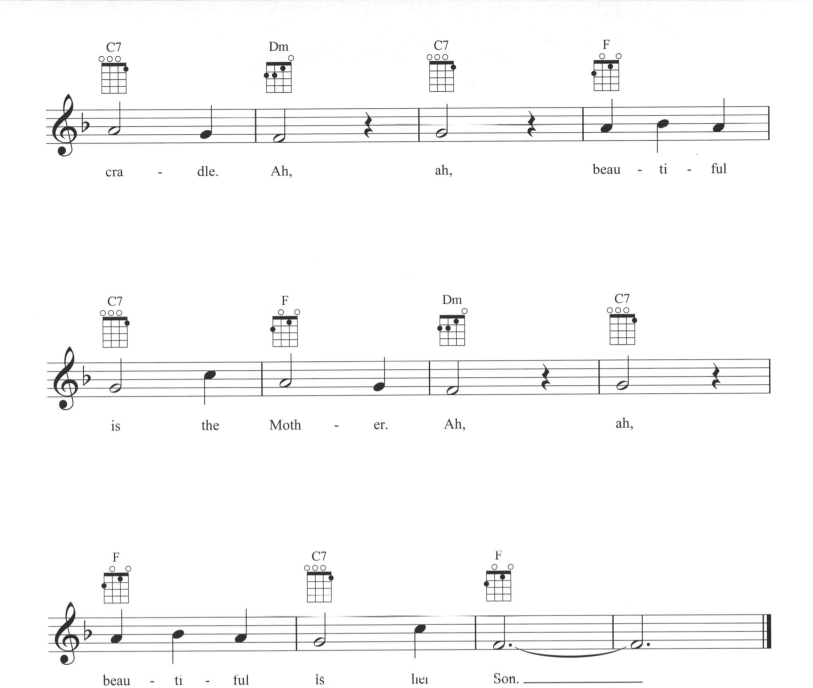

cra - dle. Ah, ah, beau - ti - ful

is the Moth - er. Ah, ah,

beau - ti - ful is her Son. _____

Additional Lyrics

2. Hasten now, good folk of the village,
Hasten now, the Christ Child to see.
You will find Him asleep in a manger,
Quietly come and whisper softly.
Hush, hush, peacefully now He slumbers,
Hush, hush, peacefully now He sleeps.

Carol of the Birds

Traditional Catalonian Carol

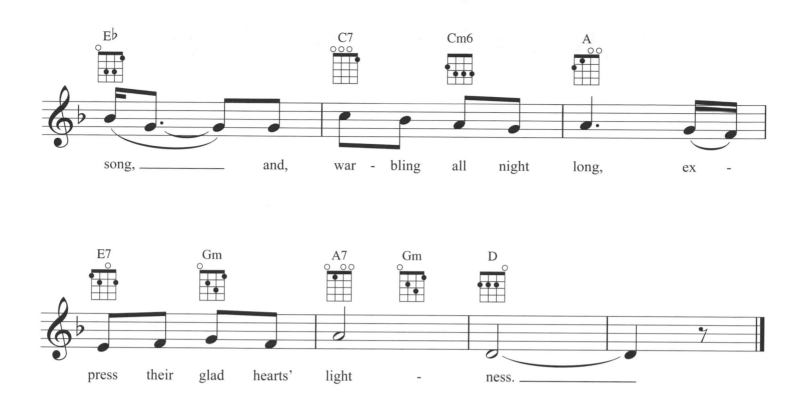

song, _____ and, war - bling all night long, ex -

press their glad hearts' light - ness. _____

Additional Lyrics

2. The Nightingale is first
   To bring his song of cheer,
   And tell us of his gladness:
   "Jesus, our Lord, is born
   To free us from all sin,
   And banish ev'ry sadness!
   Jesus, our Lord, is born
   To free us from all sin,
   And banish ev'ry sadness!"

3. The answ'ring Sparrow cries:
   "God comes to earth this day
   Amid the angels flying."
   Trilling in sweetest tones,
   The Finch his Lord now owns:
   "To Him be all thanksgiving."
   Trilling in sweetest tones,
   The Finch his Lord now owns:
   "To Him be all thanksgiving."

4. The Partridge adds his note:
   "To Bethlehem I'll fly,
   Where in the stall He's lying.
   There, near the manger blest,
   I'll build myself a nest,
   And sing my love undying.
   There, near the manger blest,
   I'll build myself a nest,
   And sing my love undying."

A Child Is Born in Bethlehem

14th-Century Latin Text adapted by Nicolai F.S. Grundtvig
Traditional Danish Melody

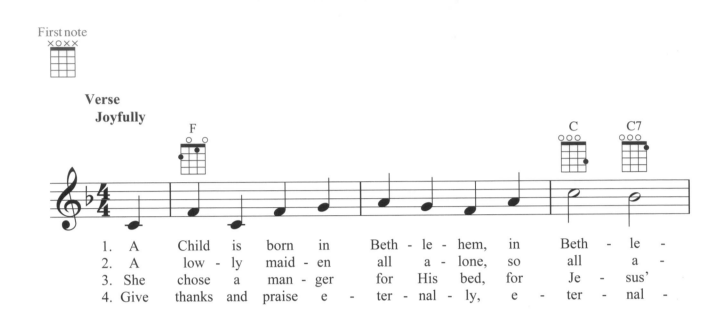

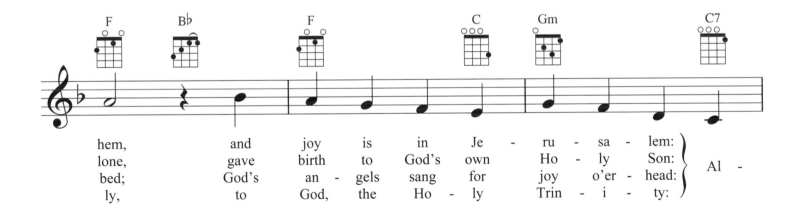

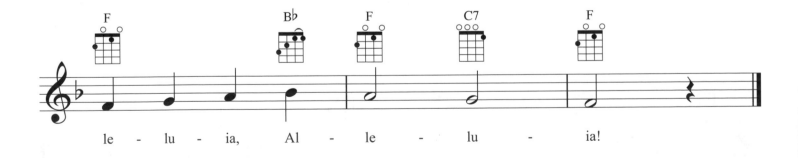

Child Jesus Came to Earth This Day

Traditional Carol

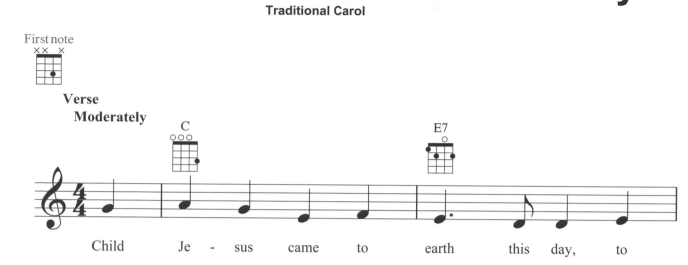

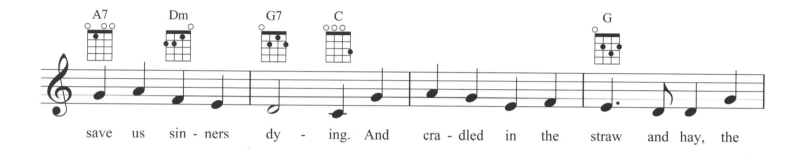

Child Je - sus came to earth this day, to

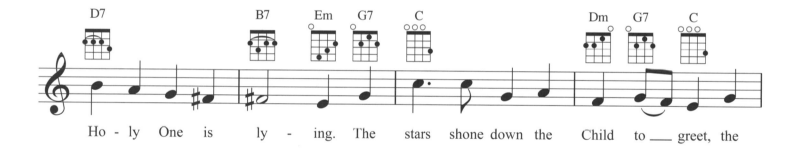

save us sin - ners dy - ing. And cra - dled in the straw and hay, the

Ho - ly One is ly - ing. The stars shone down the Child to ___ greet, the

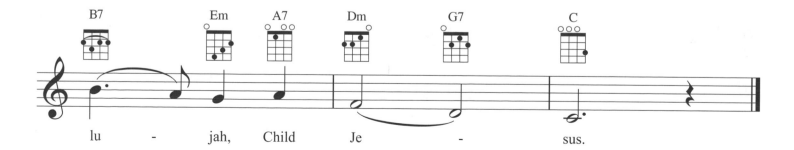

low - ing ox - en kiss the feet. Hal - le - lu - jah, Hal - le -

lu - jah, Child Je - sus.

Christ Is Born This Evening

Traditional

Christ Was Born on Christmas Day

Traditional

Christians, Awake!
Salute the Happy Morn

Words by John Byrom
Music by John Wainwright

With them the joy - ful tid - ings first be - gun Of
This day hath God ful - filled His prom - ised word; This

God In - car - nate and the Vir - gin's Son.
day is born a Sav - ior, Christ the Lord."

Additional Lyrics

3. He spake; and straightway the celestial choir
   In hymns of joy, unknown before, conspire;
   The praises of redeeming love they sang
   And heaven's whole orb with alleluias rang;
   God's highest glory was their anthem still,
   Peace upon earth, and unto men good will.

4. Then may we hope, th'angelic hosts among,
   To sing, redeemed, a glad triumphant song;
   He that was born upon this joyful day
   Around us all His glory shall display;
   Saved by His love, incessant we shall sing
   Eternal praise to heaven's Almighty King.

The Christmas Tree with Its Candles Gleaming

Traditional Czech Text
Traditional Bohemian-Czech Tune

Come, All Ye Shepherds

Traditional Czech Text
Traditional Moravian Melody

First note

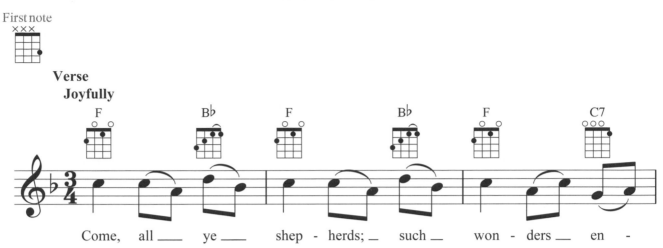

Verse
Joyfully

Come, all ye shep-herds; such won-ders en-

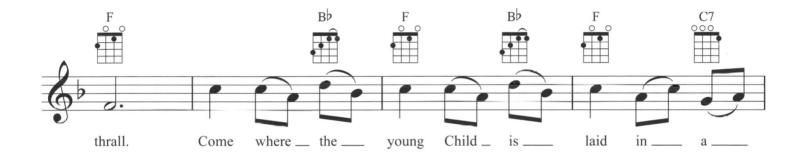

thrall. Come where the young Child is laid in a

stall. This day to us a Sav-ior is giv-en, Whom God on high hath

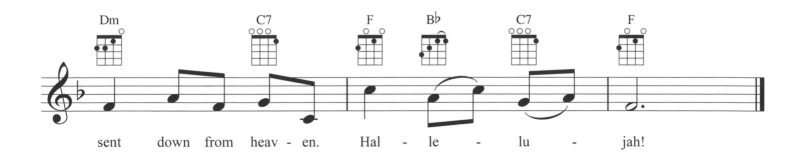

sent down from heav-en. Hal-le-lu-jah!

Come, Thou Long-Expected Jesus

Words by Charles Wesley
Music by Rowland Hugh Prichard

First note

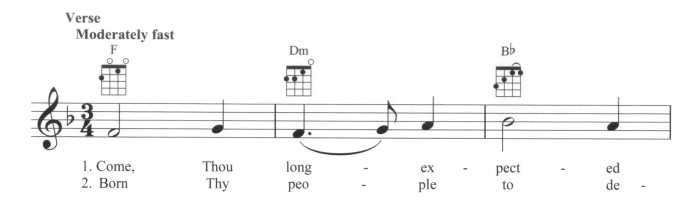

Verse
Moderately fast

1. Come, Thou long - ex - pect - ed
2. Born Thy peo - ple to de -

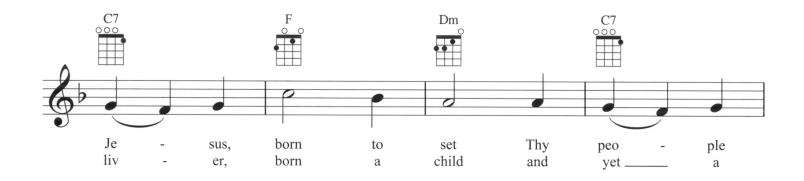

Je - sus, born to set Thy peo - ple
liv - er, born a child and yet _____ a

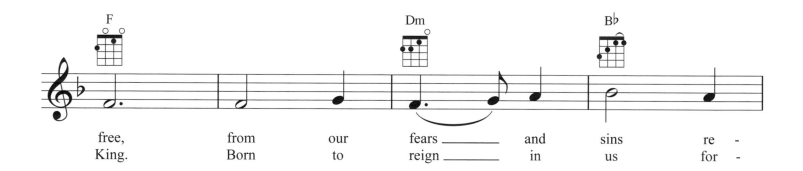

free, from our fears _____ and sins re -
King. Born to reign _____ in us for -

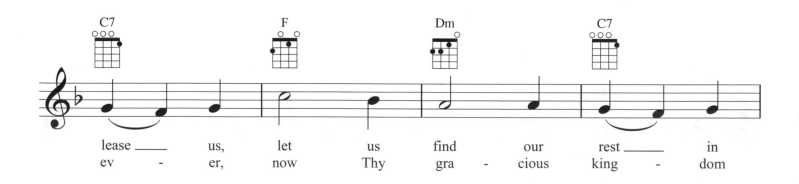

lease _____ us, let us find our rest _____ in
ev - er, now Thy gra - cious king - dom

Coventry Carol

Words by Robert Croo
Traditional English Melody

Additional Lyrics

3. Herod the king, in his raging,
   Charged he hath this day
   His men of might, in his own sight,
   All young children to slay.

4. That woe is me, poor Child, for Thee!
   And ever morn and day,
   For Thy parting neither say nor sing,
   By, by, lully, lullay.

Dance of the Sugar Plum Fairy

from THE NUTCRACKER
By Pyotr Il'yich Tchaikovsky

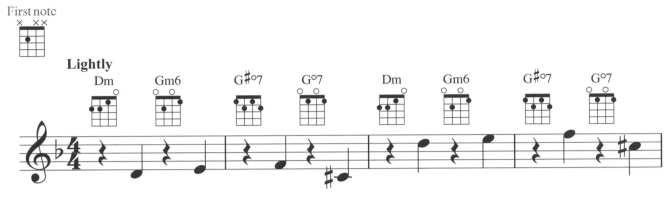

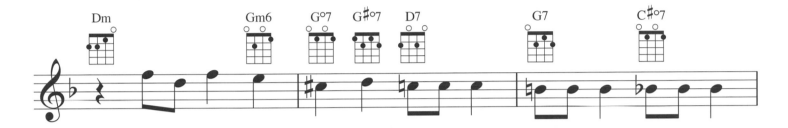

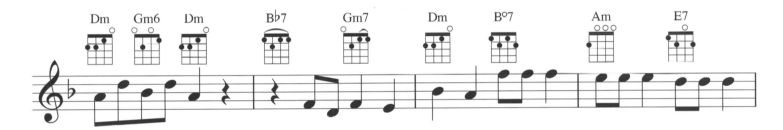

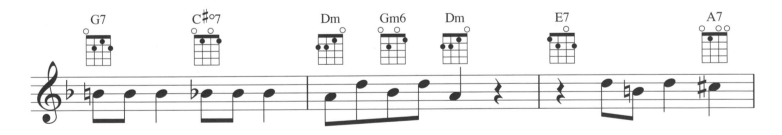

A Day, Bright Day of Glory

Traditional

First note

Verse
Moderately

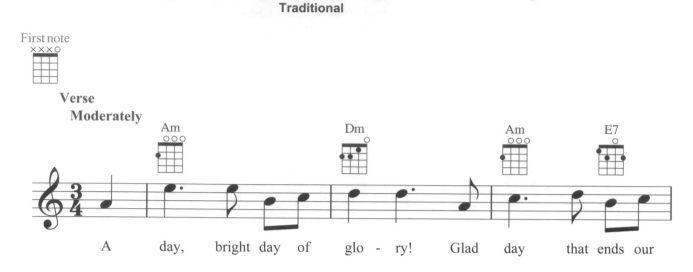

A day, bright day of glo - ry! Glad day that ends our

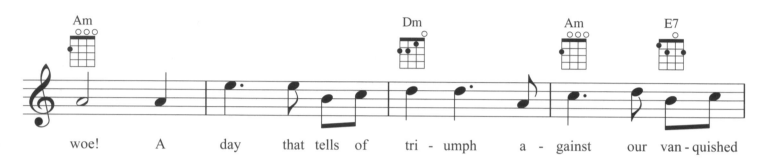

woe! A day that tells of tri - umph a - gainst our van - quished

foe! For us this Christ - mas sun - rise, this

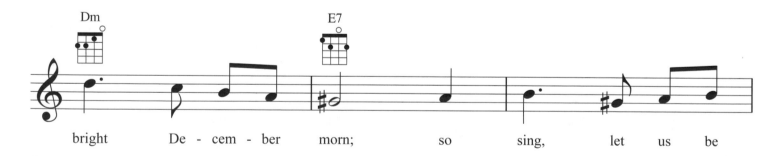

bright De - cem - ber morn; so sing, let us be

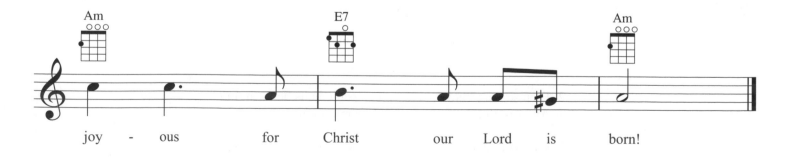

joy - ous for Christ our Lord is born!

Ding Dong! Merrily on High!

Traditional French Carol

Additional Lyrics

2. E'en so here below, below, let steeple bells be swinging.
   And i-o, i-o, i-o, by priest and people singing.

3. Pray you, dutifully prime your matin chime, ye ringers.
   May you beautiful rime your evetime song, ye singers.

Deck the Hall

Traditional Welsh Carol

First note

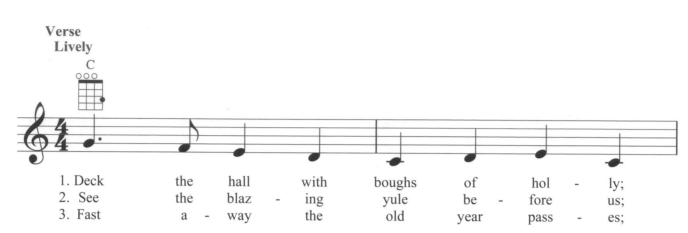

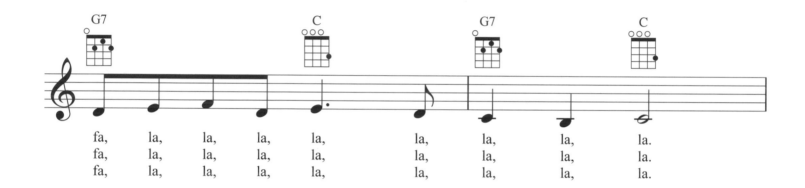

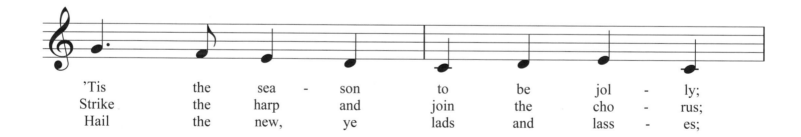

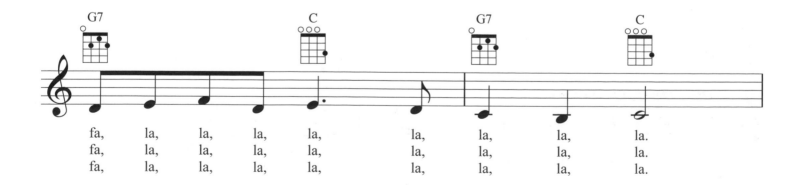

Don   we   now   our   gay   ap - par - el;
Fol - low   me   in   mer - ry   meas - ure;
Sing   we   joy - ous   all   to - geth - er;

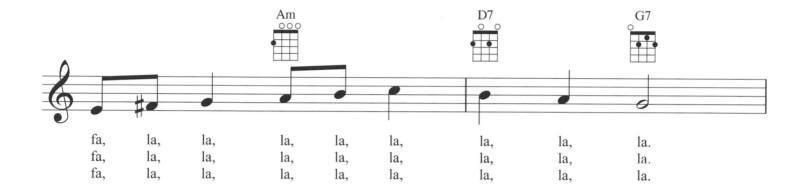

fa,   la,   la,   la,   la,   la,   la,   la,   la.
fa,   la,   la,   la,   la,   la,   la,   la,   la.
fa,   la,   la,   la,   la,   la,   la,   la,   la.

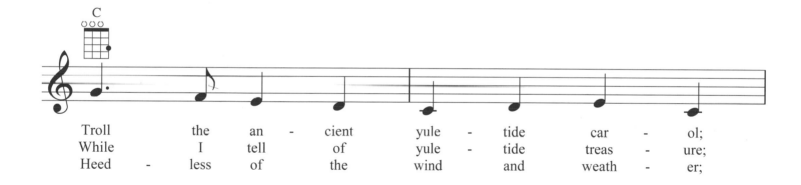

Troll   the   an - cient   yule - tide   car - ol;
While   I   tell   of   yule - tide   treas - ure;
Heed - less   of   the   wind   and   weath - er;

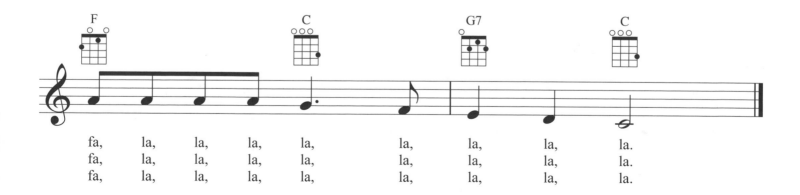

fa,   la,   la,   la,   la,   la,   la,   la,   la.
fa,   la,   la,   la,   la,   la,   la,   la,   la.
fa,   la,   la,   la,   la,   la,   la,   la,   la.

The First Noël

17th Century English Carol
Music from W. Sandys' *Christmas Carols*

1. The ___ first ___ No - ël the ___ an - gel did
(2.–5.) *See additional lyrics*

say, was to cer - tain poor shep - herds in

fields as they lay; in ___ fields ___ where ___

they lay ___ keep - ing their sheep, on a

cold win - ter's night ___ that was ___ so deep. No -

Chorus

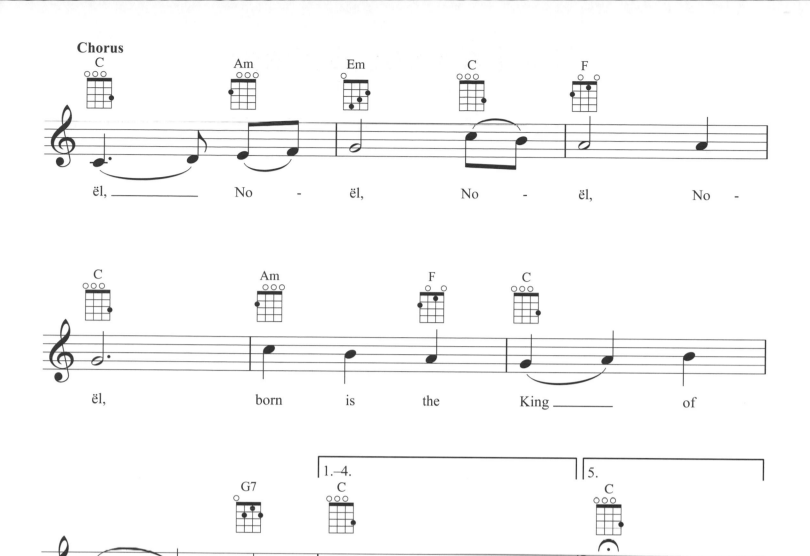

ël, _____ No - ël, No - ël, No -

ël, born is the King _____ of

Is - ra - el. 2. They ___ el.

Additional Lyrics

2. They looked up and saw a star
   Shining in the east, beyond them far;
   And to the earth it gave great light
   And so it continued both day and night.

3. And by the light of that same star,
   Three wise men came from country far;
   To seek for a King was their intent,
   And to follow the star wherever it went.

4. This star drew nigh to the northwest,
   O'er Bethlehem it took its rest;
   And there it did both stop and stay,
   Right over the place where Jesus lay.

5. Then entered in those wise men three,
   Full reverently upon their knee;
   And offered there in His presence,
   Their gold and myrrh and frankincense.

The Friendly Beasts

Traditional English Carol

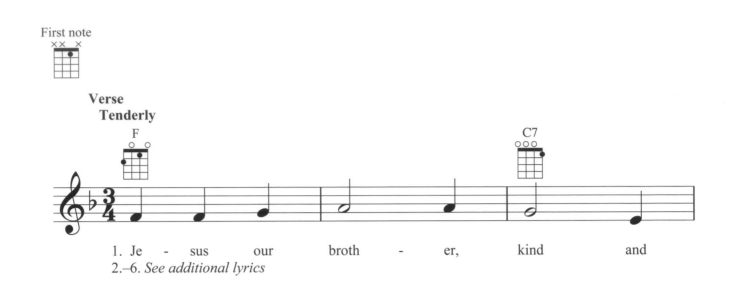

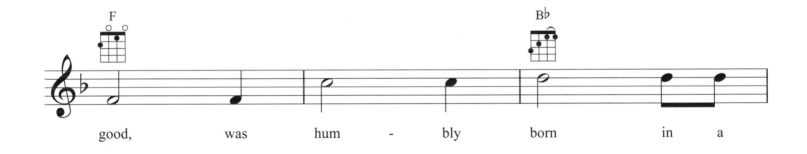

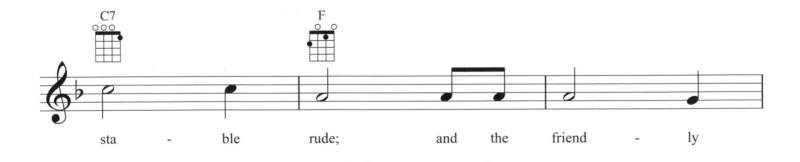

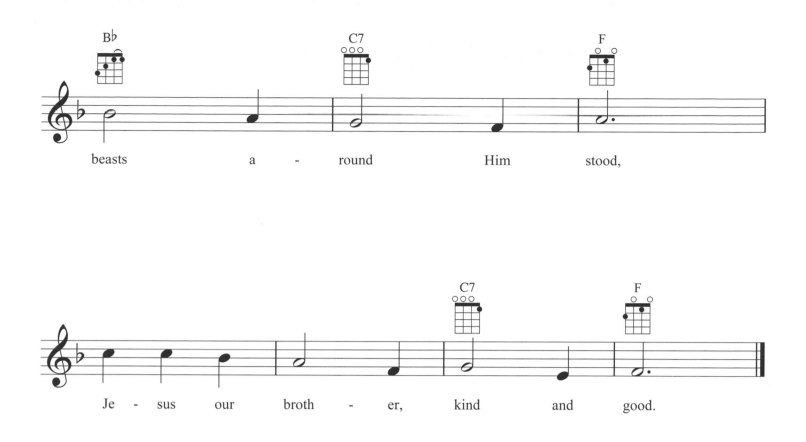

beasts   a - round   Him   stood,

Je - sus our broth - er, kind and good.

Additional Lyrics

2. "I," said the donkey, shaggy and brown,
   "I carried His mother up hill and down.
   I carried His mother to Bethlehem town."
   "I," said the donkey, shaggy and brown.

3. "I," said the cow, all white and red,
   "I gave Him my manger for His bed.
   I gave Him my hay to pillow His head."
   "I," said the cow, all white and red.

4. "I," said the sheep with the curly horn,
   "I gave Him my wool for His blanket warm.
   He wore my coat on Christmas morn."
   "I," said the sheep with the curly horn.

5. "I," said the dove from the rafters high,
   "I cooed Him to sleep that He would not cry.
   We cooed Him to sleep, my mate and I."
   "I," said the dove from the rafters high.

6. Thus every beast by some good spell,
   In the stable dark was glad to tell
   Of the gift he gave Emmanuel,
   The gift he gave Emmanuel.

From Heaven Above to Earth I Come

Words by Martin Luther
Music from *Geistliche Lieder*, 1539

Fum, Fum, Fum

Traditional Catalonian Carol

Go, Tell It on the Mountain

African-American Spiritual
Verses by John W. Work, Jr.

The Happy Christmas Comes Once More

Words by Nicolai F.S. Grundtvig
Music by C. Balle

Additional Lyrics

2. To David's city let us fly,
   Where angels sing beneath the sky,
   Through plain and village pressing near,
   And news from God with shepherds hear.

3. O let us go with quiet mind,
   The gentle Babe with shepherds find,
   To gaze on Him who gladdens them,
   The loveliest flow'r on Jesse's stem.

4. Come, Jesus, glorious heav'nly Guest,
   Keep Thine own Christmas in our breast.
   Then David's harp-string, hushed so long,
   Shall swell our jubilee of song.

God Rest Ye Merry, Gentlemen

19th Century English Carol

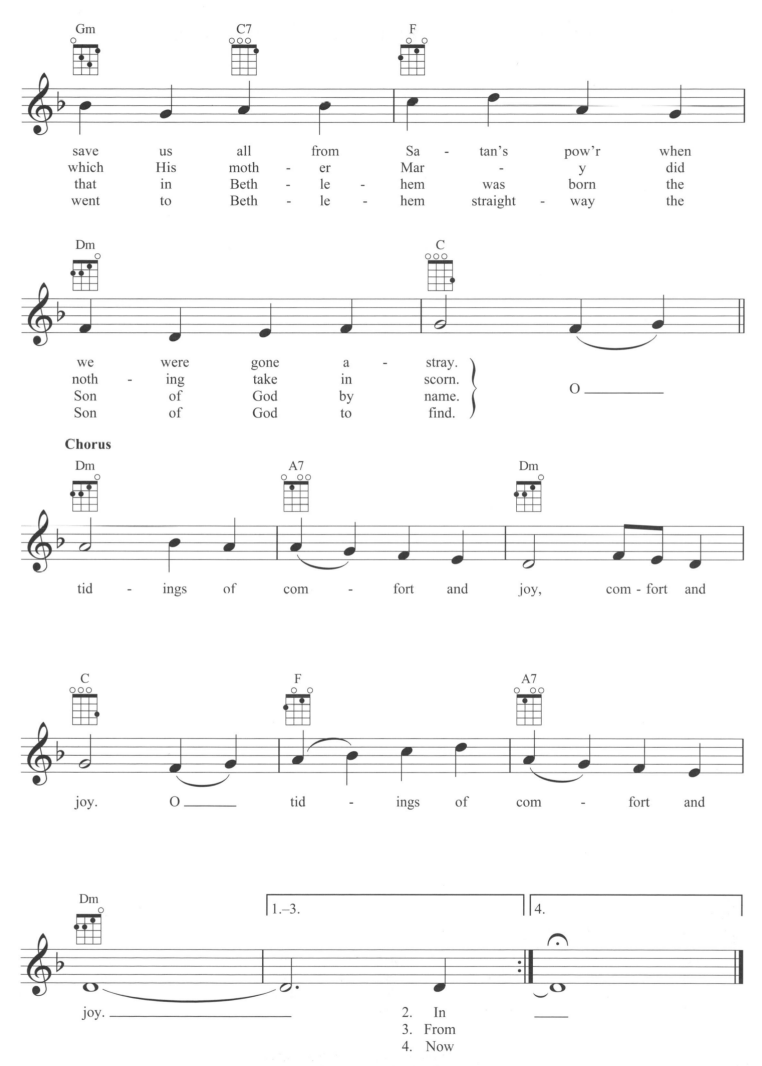

save us all from Sa - tan's pow'r when
which His moth - er Mar - y did
that in Beth - le - hem was born the
went to Beth - le - hem straight - way the

we were gone a - stray.
noth - ing take in scorn.
Son of God by name.
Son of God to find.

O _____

Chorus

tid - ings of com - fort and joy, com - fort and

joy. O _____ tid - ings of com - fort and

joy. _____

1.–3.

2. In ____
3. From
4. Now

Good Christian Men, Rejoice

14th Century Latin Text
Translated by John Mason Neale
14th Century German Melody

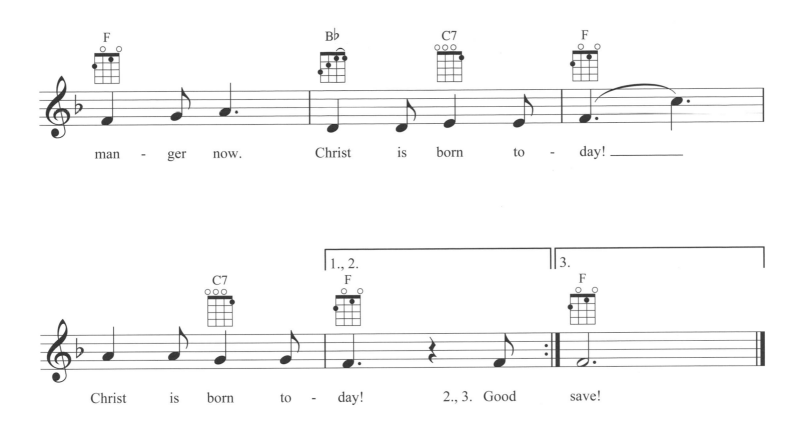

Additional Lyrics

2. Good Christian men, rejoice
   With heart and soul and voice.
   Now ye hear of endless bliss: Joy! Joy!
   Jesus Christ was born for this.
   He hath op'd the heavenly door,
   And man is blessed evermore.
   Christ was born for this!
   Christ was born for this!

3. Good Christian men, rejoice
   With heart and soul and voice.
   Now ye need not fear the grave: Peace! Peace!
   Jesus Christ was born to save!
   Calls you one and calls you all,
   To gain His everlasting hall.
   Christ was born to save!
   Christ was born to save!

Good King Wenceslas

Words by John M. Neale
Music from *Piae Cantiones*

First note

Verse
Moderately, in 2

1. Good King Wen - ces - las looked out
2. "Hith - er, page, and stand by me,
3. "Bring me flesh, and bring me wine,
4., 5. *See additional lyrics*

on the feast of Ste - phen;
if thou know'st it tell - ing;
bring me pine logs hith - er;

when the snow lay 'round a - bout,
yon - der peas - ant, who is he?
thou and I will see him dine,

deep and crisp and e - ven.
Where and what his dwell - ing?"
when we bear them thith - er."

Bright - ly shone the moon that night, though the frost was
"Sire, he lives a good league hence, un - der - neath the
Page and mon - arch forth they went, forth they went to -

cru - el; when a poor man came in sight,
moun - tain; right a - gainst the for - est fence,
geth - er; through the rude wind's wild la - ment

gath - 'ring win - ter fu - el.
by St. Ag - nes foun - tain."
and the bit - ter weath - er.

Additional Lyrics

4. "Sire, the night is darker now,
   And the wind blows stronger;
   Fails my heart, I know not how,
   I can go no longer."
   "Mark my footsteps, my good page,
   Tread thou in them boldly;
   Thou shalt find the winter's rage
   Freeze thy blood less coldly."

5. In his master's steps he trod,
   Where the snow lay dinted;
   Heat was in the very sod
   Which the saint has printed.
   Therefore, Christmas men, be sure,
   Wealth or rank possessing;
   Ye who now will bless the poor
   Shall yourselves find blessing.

Hark! The Herald Angels Sing

Words by Charles Wesley
Altered by George Whitefield
Music by Felix Mendelssohn-Bartholdy
Arranged by William H. Cummings

1. Hark! the her - ald an - gels sing, _____
2. Christ, by high - est heav'n a - dored, _____
3. Hail, the heav'n - born Prince of Peace! _____

"Glo - ry to the new - born King!
Christ, the ev - er - last - ing Lord!
Hail, the Son of right - eous - ness!

Peace on earth, and mer - cy mild, _____
Late in time be - hold Him come, _____
Light and life to all He brings, _____

God and sin - ners
off - spring of the
ris'n with heal - ing

rec - on - ciled." Joy - ful, all ye na - tions rise, _____
vir - gin's womb. Veil'd in flesh the God - head see, _____
in His wings. Mild He lays His glo - ry by, _____

Chorus

He Is Born, the Holy Child

(Il est ne, le divin enfant)

Traditional French Carol

First note

Chorus
Moderately, in 2

He is born, the ___ Ho - ly Child.

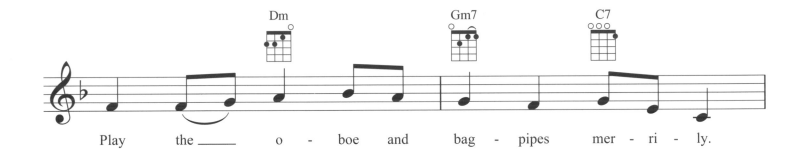

Play the ___ o - boe and bag - pipes mer - ri - ly.

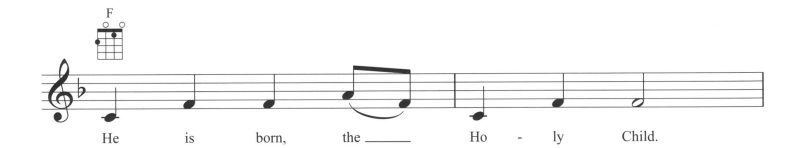

He is born, the ___ Ho - ly Child.

Fine

Sing we all of the Sav - ior's birth.

Verse

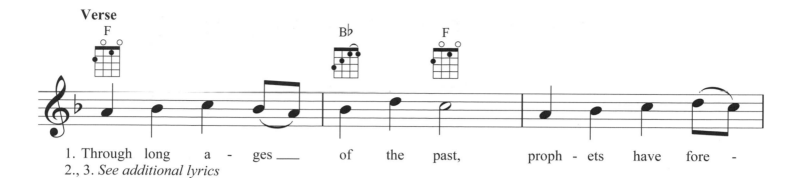

1. Through long a - ges ____ of the past, proph - ets have fore -
2., 3. *See additional lyrics*

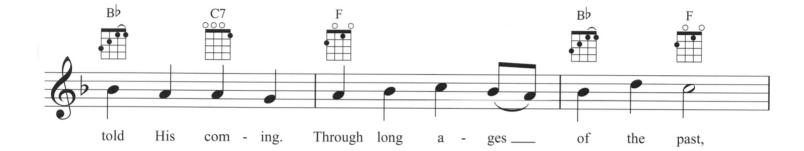

told His com - ing. Through long a - ges ____ of the past,

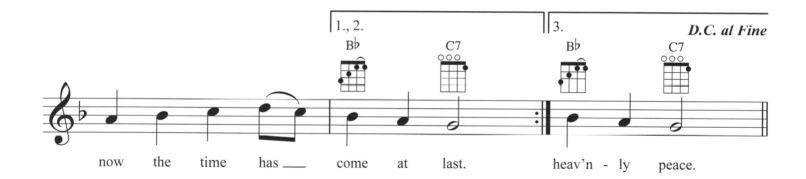

D.C. al Fine

1., 2.

now the time has ____ come at last.

3.

heav'n - ly peace.

Additional Lyrics

2. Oh, how lovely, oh, how pure,
   Is this perfect Child of heaven.
   Oh, how lovely, oh, how pure,
   Gracious gift of God to man.

3. Jesus, Lord of all the world,
   Coming as a child among us.
   Jesus, Lord of all the world,
   Grant to us Thy heav'nly peace.

Here We Come A-Wassailing

Traditional

First note

Verse
Brightly

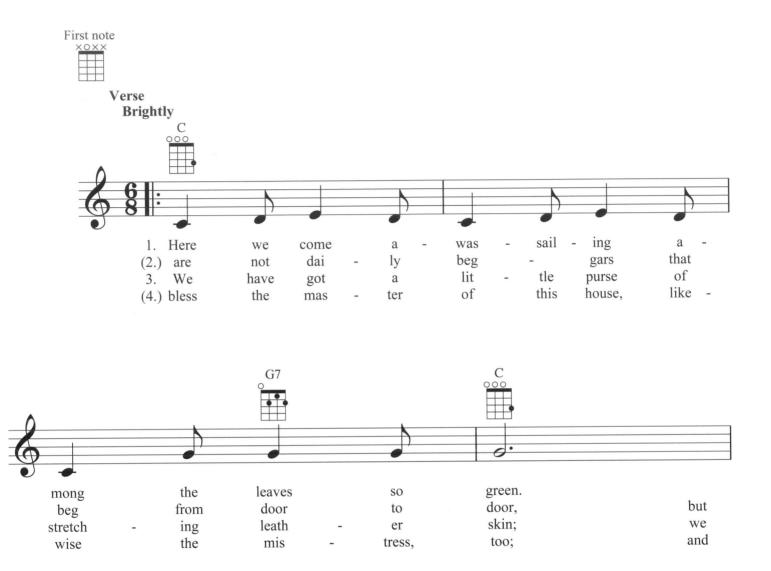

1. Here we come a - was - sail - ing a -
(2.) are we not dai - ly beg - gars that
3. We have got a lit - tle purse of
(4.) bless the mas - ter of this house, like -

mong the leaves so green.
beg from door to door, but
stretch - ing leath - er skin; we
wise the mis - tress, too; and

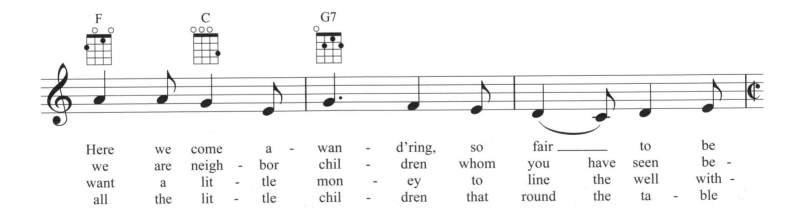

Here we come a - wan - d'ring, so fair _____ to be
we are neigh - bor chil - dren whom you have seen be -
want a lit - tle mon - ey to line the well with -
all the lit - tle chil - dren that round the ta - ble

The Holly and the Ivy

18th Century English Carol

Additional Lyrics

2. The holly bears a blossom
   As white as lily flow'r,
   And Mary bore sweet Jesus Christ,
   To be our sweet Savior.

3. The holly bears a berry
   As red as any blood,
   And Mary bore sweet Jesus Christ,
   To do poor sinners good.

I Am So Glad on Christmas Eve

Words by Marie Wexelsen
Music by Peder Knudsen

I Heard the Bells on Christmas Day

Words by Henry Wadsworth Longfellow
Music by John Baptiste Calkin

Additional Lyrics

3. And in despair I bowed my head:
   "There is no peace on earth," I said,
   "For hate is strong, and mocks the song
   Of peace on earth, good will to men."

4. Then pealed the bells more loud and deep:
   "God is not dead, nor doth He sleep;
   The wrong shall fail, the right prevail,
   With peace on earth, good will to men."

5. Till ringing, singing on its way,
   The world revolved from night to day,
   A voice, a chime, a chant sublime,
   Of peace on earth, good will to men!

I Saw Three Ships

Traditional English Carol

In the Field with Their Flocks Abiding

Traditional

First note

Verse
Moderately

F

In the field with their flocks a - bid - ing, they __

C7   F

lay on the dew - y ground. And __ glim - m'ring __ un - der the

C7   F

star - light, the __ sheep lay white a - round; when the

Dm   G7   Em7   Am

light of the Lord streamed o'er _____ them, and

lo! from the heav - en a - bove, an an - gel leaned from the

glo - ry and sang his song of love. He

Chorus

sang that first sweet Christ - mas, the

song that shall nev - er cease: "Glo - ry to God in the

high - est, on earth good - will and peace!"

In the Silence of the Night

Traditional Carol

Jesus Holy, Born So Lowly

Traditional Polish

First note

Verse
Like a lullaby

1. Je - sus ho - ly, born so low - ly,
2. On the straw the Babe is sleep - ing

we will sing you car - ols gay. Je - sus dear - est,
in the hum - ble man - ger bed. Mar - y lov - ing

pre - cious In - fant, come to us from Heav'n to - day.
watch is keep - ing, an - gels hov - er 'round His head.

Chorus

Shep - herds, join the joy - ful cho - rus; heav'n - ly love is
Shep - herds, how in ad - o - ra - tion, prais - ing God's sweet

reign - ing o'er ___ us, here ap - pear - ing as a Babe.
be - ne - dic - tion that up - on the earth is shed.

It Came Upon the Midnight Clear

Words by Edmund Hamilton Sears
Music by Richard Storrs Willis

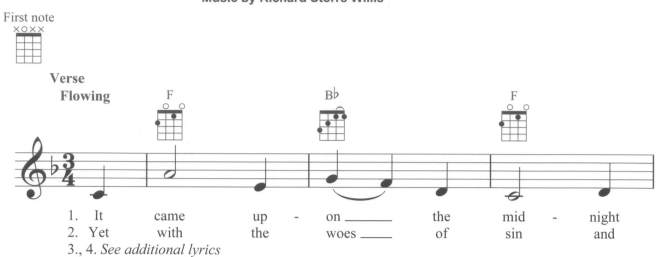

First note

Verse
Flowing

1. It came up - on _____ the mid - night
2. Yet with the woes _____ of sin and
3., 4. *See additional lyrics*

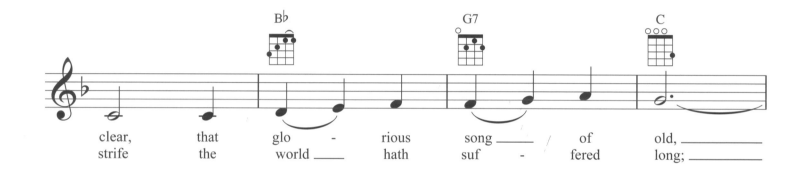

clear, that glo - rious song _____ / of old, _____
strife the world _____ hath suf - fered long; _____

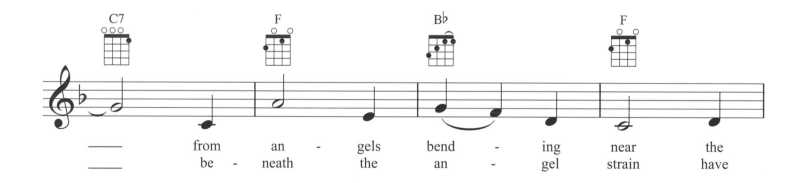

_____ from an - gels bend - ing near the
_____ be - neath the an - gel strain have

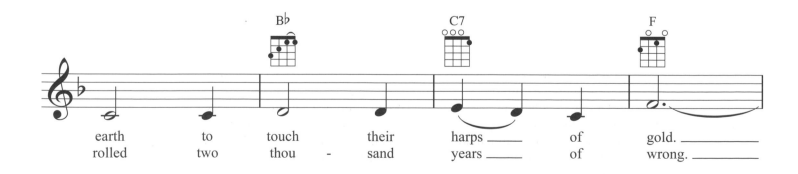

earth to touch their harps _____ of gold. _____
rolled to two thou - sand years _____ of wrong. _____

Additional Lyrics

3. And ye, beneath life's crushing load,
   Whose forms are bending low,
   Who toil along the climbing way
   With painful steps and slow;
   Look now, for glad and golden hours
   Come swiftly on the wing.
   O rest beside the weary road
   And hear the angels sing.

4. For lo, the days are hast'ning on,
   By prophet bards foretold,
   When with the ever-circling years
   Comes round the age of gold;
   When peace shall over all the earth
   Its ancient splendors fling,
   And the whole world give back the song
   Which now the angels sing.

Jesu, Joy of Man's Desiring

English Words by Robert Bridges
Music by Johann Sebastian Bach

First note

Verse
Moderately

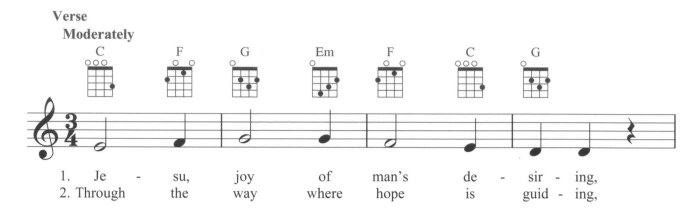

1. Je - su, joy of man's de - sir - ing,
2. Through the way where hope is guid - ing,

ho - ly wis - dom, love _____ most _____ bright.
hark, what peace - ful mu - sic _____ rings!

Drawn by Thee, our souls as - pir - ing,
Where the flock in Thee con - fid - ing,

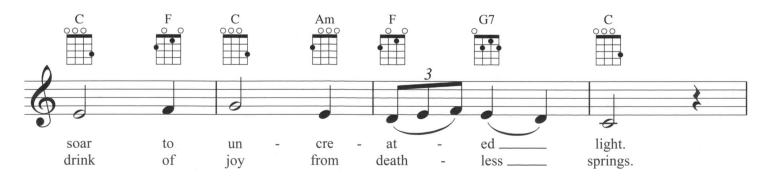

soar to un - cre - at - ed _____ light.
drink of joy from death - less _____ springs.

Word of God, our flesh _____ that fash - ioned,
Theirs is beau - ty's fair - est pleas - ure,

with the fire of life _____ im - pas - sioned.
theirs is wis - dom's ho - licst treas - ure.

Striv - ing still to truth un - known,
Thou dost ev - er truth lead Thine own,

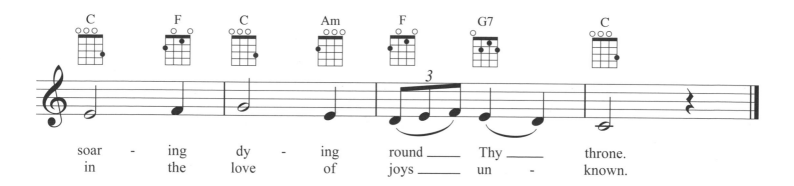

soar - ing dy - ing round _____ Thy _____ throne.
in the dy love of joys _____ un - known.

Joy to the World

Words by Isaac Watts
Music by George Frideric Handel
Adapted by Lowell Mason

Lo, How a Rose E'er Blooming

15th Century German Carol
Translated by Theodore Baker
Music from *Alte Catholische Geistliche Kirchengesang*

Masters in This Hall

Traditional English Carol

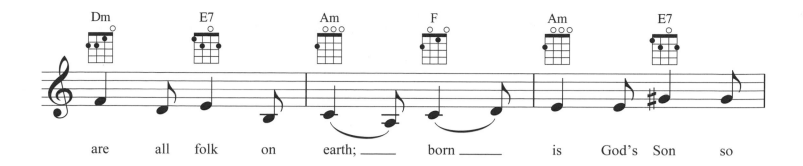

are   all   folk   on   earth; ____ born ____ is   God's   Son   so

dear.   No - ël!   No - ël!   No - ël!

No - ël   sing   we   loud!   God   to - day   hath   all   folk

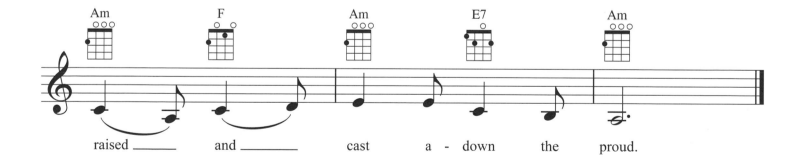

raised ____ and ____ cast   a - down   the   proud.

Additional Lyrics

4. And a little child
   On her arm had she.
   "Wot ye who this is?"
   Said the hinds to me.

5. This is Christ the Lord;
   Masters, be ye glad.
   Christmas is come in
   And no folk should be sad.

Neighbor, What Has You So Excited?

Traditional French

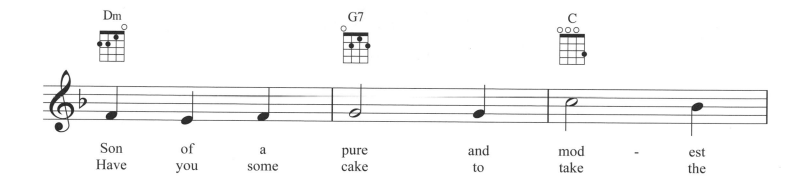

Son of a pure and mod - est
Have you a some cake to take the

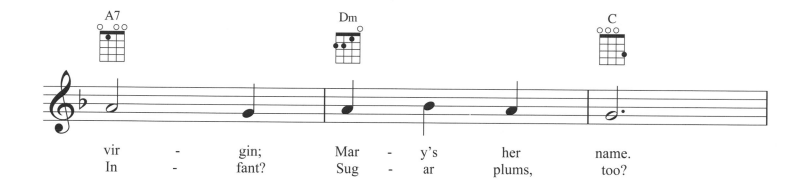

vir - gin; Mar - y's her name.
In - fant? Sug - ar her plums, too?

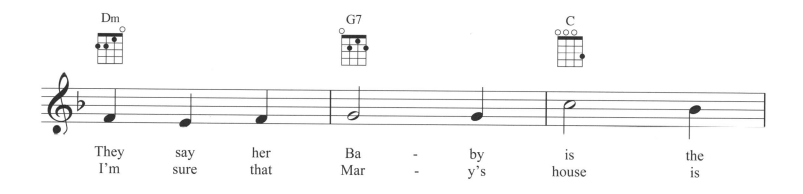

They say her Ba - by is the
I'm sure that her Mar - y's house is

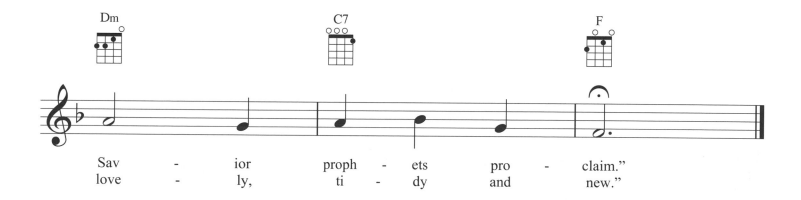

Sav - ior proph - ets pro - claim."
love - ly, ti - dy and new."

Noël! Noël!

French-English Carol

O Bethlehem

Traditional Spanish

First note

Verse
Slowly, with expression

O Beth - le - hem, o'er you a bril - liant star is shin - ing, O Beth - le - hem. Heav - en - ly choirs of an - gels bring to ___ the world glad news of an in - fant King. 'Round you the hills and val - leys are ech - o - ing! O Beth - le - hem, ___ O Beth - le - hem.

O Christmas Tree

Traditional German Carol

O Come, All Ye Faithful

Music by John Francis Wade
Latin Words translated by Frederick Oakeley

O Come Away, Ye Shepherds

18th Century French Text
Tune from Air, "Nanon Dormait"

change your tears to praise and ju - bi -
heav'n a - bove He comes to earth to

la - tion! We jour - ney to a -
save us as God's In - car - nate

dore a God, (a God,) a
Word. He is, (He is,) He

God (a God) who brings us con - so -
is (He is) our Lord and faith - ful

la - tion.
Shep - herd.

2. O

O Come, Little Children

Words by C. von Schmidt
Music by J.P.A. Schulz

First note

Quietly   Verse

1. O come, lit - tle chil - dren, from cot and from
(2.) "Glo - ry to God!" sing the an - gels on

hall. O come to the man - ger in Beth - le - hem's stall. There
high, and "Peace up - on earth!" heav'n - ly voic - es re - ply. Then

meek - ly He ly - eth, the heav - en - ly Child, so
come lit - tle chil - dren, and join in the day that

poor and so hum - ble, so sweet and so mild. 2. Now,
glad - dened the world on that first Christ - mas

Day.

O Come, O Come, Immanuel

Plainsong, 13th Century
Words translated by John M. Neale and Henry S. Coffin

O Come Rejoicing

Traditional Polish Carol

Chorus

Tru - ly He com - eth, Christ, our sal - va - tion.

An - gels are voic - ing their ju - bi - la - tion.

Shep - herds come to praise Him, ox - en kneel be - fore Him;

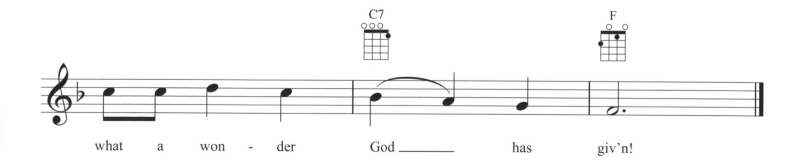

what a won - der God _____ has giv'n!

O Holy Night

French Words by Placide Cappeau
English Words by John S. Dwight
Music by Adolphe Adam

O Let Us All Be Glad Today

Words by Martin Luther
Music from *Geistliche Lieder*, 1539

First note

Additional Lyrics

3. Twice welcome, O Thou heavenly guest,
   To save a world with sin distressed.
   Com'st Thou in lowly guise for me?
   What homage shall I give to Thee?

4. Ah! Lord eternal, heavenly King,
   Hast Thou become so mean a thing?
   And hast Thou left Thy blissful seat
   To rest where colts and oxen eat?

5. Jesus, my Savior, come to me;
   Make here a little crib for Thee.
   A bed make in this heart of mine,
   That I may ay remember Thine.

6. Then from my soul glad songs shall ring;
   Of Thee each day I'll gladly sing.
   Then glad hosannas will I raise
   From heart that loves to sing Thy praise.

O Little Town of Bethlehem

Words by Phillips Brooks
Music by Lewis H. Redner

1. O lit - tle town of Beth - le - hem, how still we __ see thee lie! A - bove thy deep and dream - less sleep, the si - lent __ stars go by. Yet in thy dark streets shin - eth the ev - er - last - ing light. The hopes and fears of all the years are met in thee to - night.

2. For Christ is born of Mar - y, and gath - ered __ all a - bove, while mor - tals sleep, the an - gels keep their watch of __ won - d'ring love. O morn - ing stars to - geth - er pro - claim the ho - ly birth. And prais - es sing to God the King, and peace to men on earth.

3. O ho - ly Child of Beth - le - hem, de - scend to __ us, we pray. Cast out our sin and en - ter in, be born in __ us to - day. We hear the Christ - mas an - gels, the great glad tid - ings tell. O come to us, a - bide with us, our Lord, Im - man - u - el!

O Sanctissima

Sicilian Carol

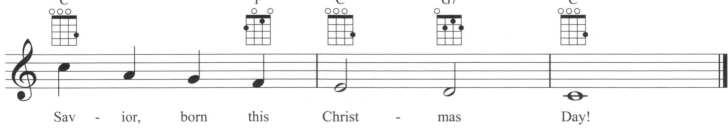

Once in Royal David's City

Words by Cecil F. Alexander
Music by Henry J. Gauntlett

1. Once in roy - al Da - vid's cit - y, stood a low - ly
2.–4. *See additional lyrics*

cat - tle shed, where a moth - er laid her ba - by

in a man - ger for His bed. Mar - y was that

moth - er mild, Je - sus Christ her lit - tle child.

Additional Lyrics

2. He came down to earth from heaven,
Who is God and Lord of all,
And His shelter was a stable,
And His cradle was a stall.
With the poor, the mean and lowly,
Lived on earth our Savior holy.

3. Jesus is our childhood's pattern;
Day by day like us He grew.
He was little, weak and helpless;
Tears and smiles, like us, He knew.
And He feeleth for our sadness,
And He shareth in our gladness.

4. And our eyes at last shall see Him,
Through His own redeeming love,
For that child so dear and gentle
Is our Lord in heav'n above.
And He leads His children on
To the place where He is gone.

Of the Father's Love Begotten

Words by Aurelius C. Prudentius
Translated by John M. Neale and Henry W. Baker
13th Century Plainsong
Arranged by C. Winfred Douglas

First note

Verse
Moderately slow

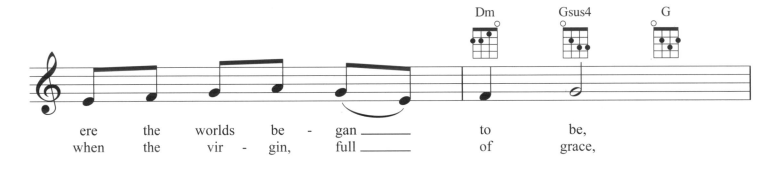

1. Of the Fa - ther's love be - got - ten,
2. O that birth for - ev - er bless - ed,
3.–5. *See additional lyrics*

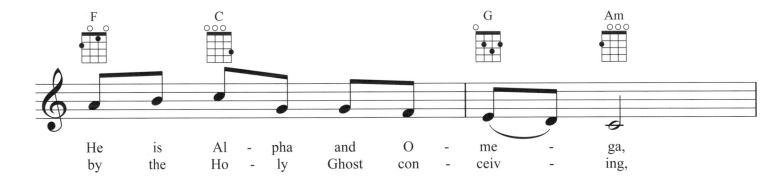

ere the worlds be - gan _____ to be,
when the vir - gin, full _____ of grace,

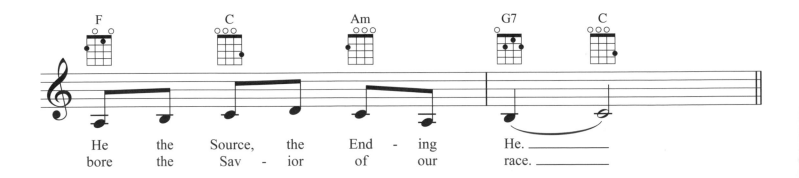

He is Al - pha and O - me - ga,
by the Ho - ly Ghost con - ceiv - ing,

He the Source, the End - ing He. _____
bore the Sav - ior of our race. _____

Chorus

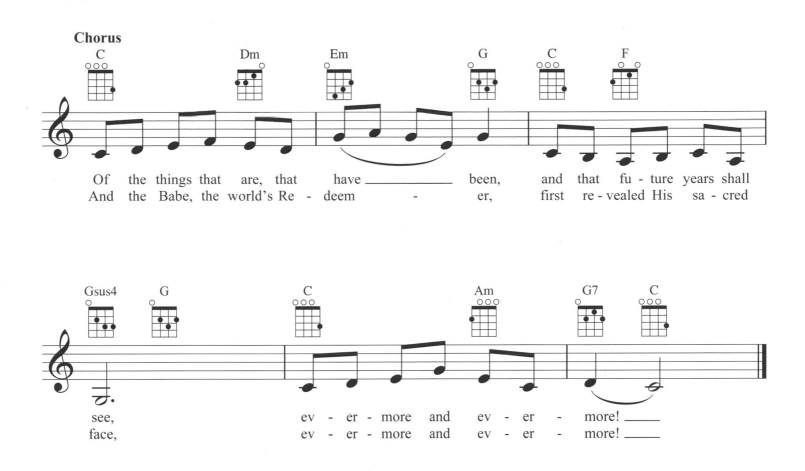

Of the things that are, that have _____ been, and that fu - ture years shall
And the Babe, the world's Re - deem - er, first re - vealed His sa - cred

see, ev - er - more and ev - er - more! _____
face, ev - er - more and ev - er - more! _____

Additional Lyrics

3. This is He whom seers in old time
   Chanted of with one accord,
   Whom the voices of the prophets
   Promised in their faithful word.

Chorus: Now He shines, the long-expected;
   Let creation praise its Lord
   Evermore and evermore!

4. Let the heights of heav'n adore Him;
   Angel hosts, his praises sing.
   Pow'rs, dominions, bow before Him
   And extol our God and King.

Chorus: Let no tongue on earth be silent;
   Ev'ry voice in concert ring
   Evermore and evermore!

5. Christ, to Thee, with God the Father,
   And, O Holy Ghost, to Thee,
   Hymn and chant and high thanksgiving
   And unwearied praises be:

Chorus: Honor, glory and dominion
   And eternal victory
   Evermore and evermore!

On Christmas Night

Sussex Carol

Chorus

News of great joy ____ and of ____ great
An - gels great and men ____ with joy ____ may

mirth, tid - ings of our dear
sing of blest Je - sus, their

| 1.–3. | 4. |

Sav - ior's birth. ____ 2. The ____
new - born King. ____ 3. So
4. From

Additional Lyrics

3. So how on earth can men be sad,
   When Jesus comes to make us glad?
   So how on earth can men be sad,
   When Jesus comes to make us glad?
   From all our sins to set us free,
   Buying for us our liberty.

4. From out the darkness have we light,
   Which makes the angels sing this night.
   From out the darkness have we light,
   Which makes the angels sing this night:
   "Glory to God, His peace to men,
   And good will, evermore! Amen."

Pat-A-Pan
(Willie, Take Your Little Drum)

Words and Music by Bernard de la Monnoye

First note

Spirited, in 2

Verse

1. Wil - lie, take your lit - tle drum. Rob - in, bring your flute and
(2.) men of old - en days gave the King of kings their
(3.) man to - day be - come close - ly joined as flute and

come. Aren't they fun to play up - on? Tu - re - lu - re -
praise, they had fun pipes to play up - on. Tu - re - lu - re -
drum. Let the joy - ous tune play on! Tu - re - lu - re -

lu, pat - a - pat - a - pan. When you play your fife and
lu, pat - a - pat - a - pan. And al - so the drums they'd
lu, pat - a - pat - a - pan. As the in - stru - ments you

1., 2. | **3.**

drum, how can an - y - one be glum? 2. When the
play, full of joy on ___ Christ - mas Day. 3. God and
play, we will sing this ___ Christ - mas

Day.

Shepherds, Shake Off Your Drowsy Sleep

Traditional French Carol

Rejoice and Be Merry

Traditional English Carol

First note

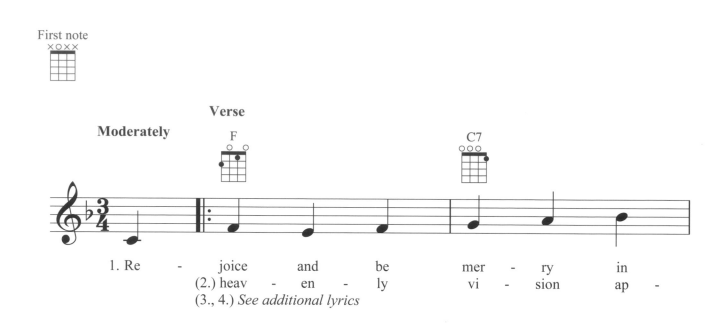

Moderately **Verse**

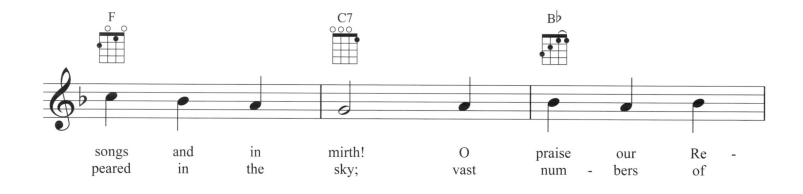

1. Re - joice and be mer - ry in
(2.) heav - en - ly vi - sion ap -
(3., 4.) *See additional lyrics*

songs and in mirth! O praise our Re -
peared in in the sky; O vast num - bers of

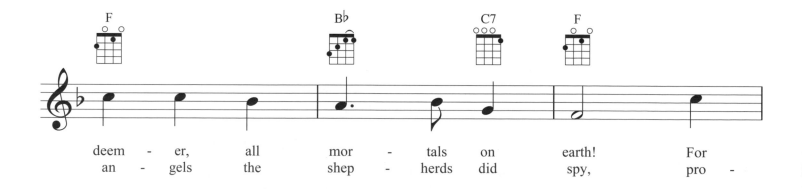

deem - er, all mor - tals on earth! For
an - gels all the shep - herds did spy, pro -

this   is   the   birth - day   of   Je - sus   our
claim - ing   the   birth - day   of   Je - sus   our

King,   who   brought   us   sal - va - tion;   His
King,   who   brought   us   sal - va - tion;   His

1.–3.   **4.**

prais - es   we'll   sing!   2. A   sing!
prais - es   we'll   sing!   3. Like -
                                   4. And

Additional Lyrics

3. Likewise, a bright star in the sky did appear,
   Which led the wise men from the east to draw near.
   They found the Messiah, sweet Jesus our King,
   Who brought us salvation; His praises we'll sing!

4. And when they were come, they their treasures unfold,
   And unto Him offered myrrh, incense and gold.
   So blessed forever be Jesus our King,
   Who brought us salvation; His praises we'll sing!

Ring Out, Ye Wild and Merry Bells

Words and Music by C. Maitland

1. Ring out, ye wild and mer - ry bells, ring
(2.) out, ye sil - v'ry bells, ring out, ring

out _____ the old, _____ old sto - ry that
out _____ your ex - ul - ta - tion that

first was told by an - gel tongues from out the realms of
God with man is rec - on - ciled. Go tell it to the

glo - ry. Peace on earth was their sweet song;
na - tions. There - fore, let us all to - day

glo - ry in the high - est! Ech - o - ing all the
glo - ry in the high - est! Ban - ish sor - row

hills a - way, glo - ry in the high - est!
far a - way, glo - ry in the high - est!

Chorus

Ring, sweet bells, ring ev - er - more, peal from ev - 'ry

stee - ple. Christ the Lord shall be our God and

1.
we ____ shall be His peo - ple! 2. Ring

2.
peo - ple!

Rise Up, Shepherd, and Follow

African-American Spiritual

fol - low. _____ Leave your sheep and leave your rams.

Rise up, shep - herd, and fol - low. _____

Chorus

Fol - low, fol - low. Rise up, shep - herd, and

fol - low. _____ Fol - low the star of Beth - le - hem. _____

1.
Rise up, shep-herd, and fol - low.

2.
2. If you fol - low. _____

Shepherds' Cradle Song

Words and Music by C.D. Schubert

First note

Flowing

Verse

1. Sleep well, Thou love - ly, heav'n - ly
(2.) well, while Mar - y holds Thee

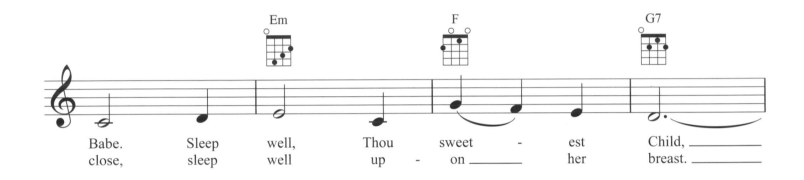

Babe. Sleep well, Thou sweet - est Child, _____
close, sleep well well up - on _____ her breast. _____

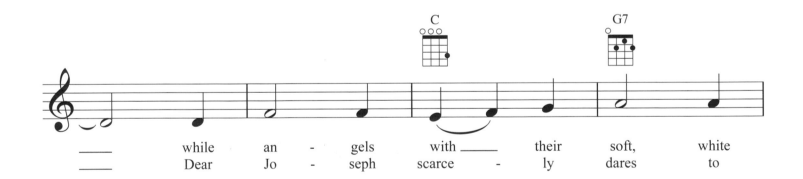

_____ while an - gels with _____ their soft, white
Dear Jo - seph scarce - ly dares to

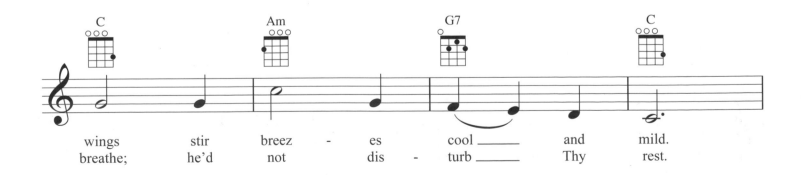

wings stir breez - es cool _____ and mild.
breathe; he'd not dis - turb _____ Thy rest.

We shep - herds poor will sing to
The lambs stand mute a - bout to the

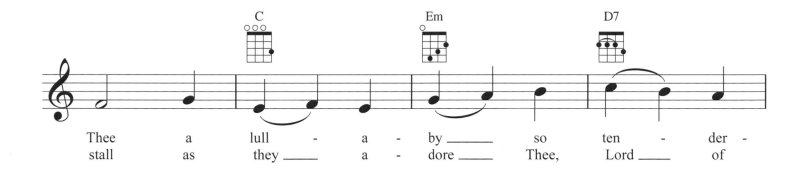

Thee a lull - a - by _____ so ten - der -
stall as they _____ a - dore _____ Thee, Lord _____ of

Chorus

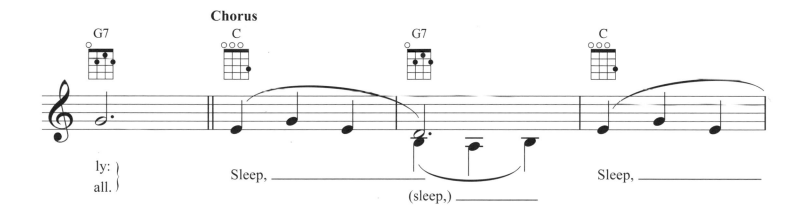

ly: }
all. }   Sleep, _____   Sleep, _____
                    (sleep,) _____

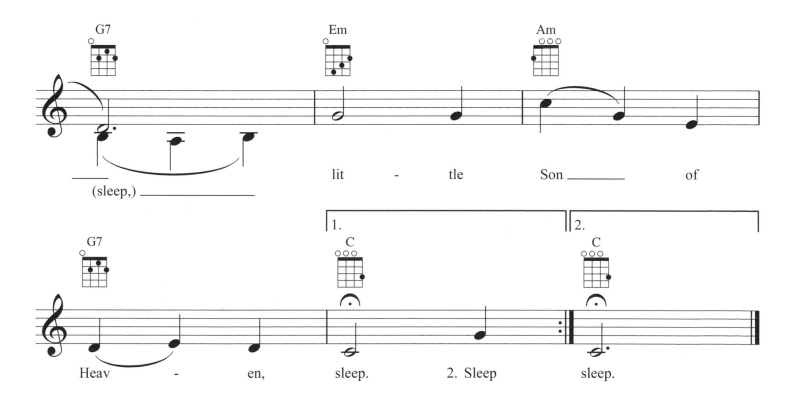

_____ (sleep,) _____   lit - tle Son _____ of

1.   2.

Heav - en, sleep.   2. Sleep   sleep.

Shout the Glad Tidings

Words by William Mühlenberg
Music by Charles Avison

Silent Night

Words by Joseph Mohr
Translated by John F. Young
Music by Franz X. Gruber

First note

Verse
Slowly

1. Si - lent night, ho - ly night! All is calm,
2. Si - lent night, ho - ly night! Shep - herds quake
3. Si - lent night, ho - ly night! Son of God,

all is bright 'round yon Vir - gin Moth - er and Child.
at the bright sight. Glo - ries stream ___ from heav - en a - far.
love's pure light. Ra - diant beams ___ from Thy ho - ly face

Ho - ly In - fant so ten - der and mild, sleep in heav - en - ly
Heav'n - ly hosts ___ sing Al - le - lu - ia, Christ the Sav - ior is
with the dawn of re - deem - ing grace, Je - sus, Lord, at Thy

peace. ___ Sleep ___ in heav - en - ly peace. ___
born! ___ Christ ___ the Sav - ior is born! ___
birth, ___ Je - sus, Lord, at Thy birth. ___

The Simple Birth

Traditional Flemish Carol

Additional Lyrics

3. His eyes of blackest jet were sparkling with light, *(Repeat)*
   Rosy cheeks bloomed on His face fair and bright. *(Repeat)*

4. And from His lovely mouth, the laughter did swell, *(Repeat)*
   When He saw Mary, whom He loved so well. *(Repeat)*

5. He came to weary earth, so dark and so drear, *(Repeat)*
   To wish mankind a blessed New Year. *(Repeat)*

Sing, O Sing, This Blessed Morn

Words by Christopher Wordsworth
Traditional German Tune

Lyrics (as set in score)

1. Sing, O sing, this bless-ed morn; un-to us a Child is born. Un-to us a Son is giv'n, God Him-self comes down from heav'n.

2. God with us, Im-man-u-el, reigns for-ev-er now to dwell. And on Ad-am's fall-en race, sheds the full-ness of His grace.

Sing, O sing, this bless-ed morn. Je-sus Christ to-day is born.

Additional Lyrics

3. God comes down that man may rise,
   Lifted by Him to the skies.
   Christ is Son of Man that we,
   Son of God in Him may be.

4. O renew us, Lord, we pray,
   With Thy spirit day by day,
   That we ever one may be
   With the Father and with Thee.

Sing We Now of Christmas

Traditional French Carol

First note

Verse
Joyfully, in 2

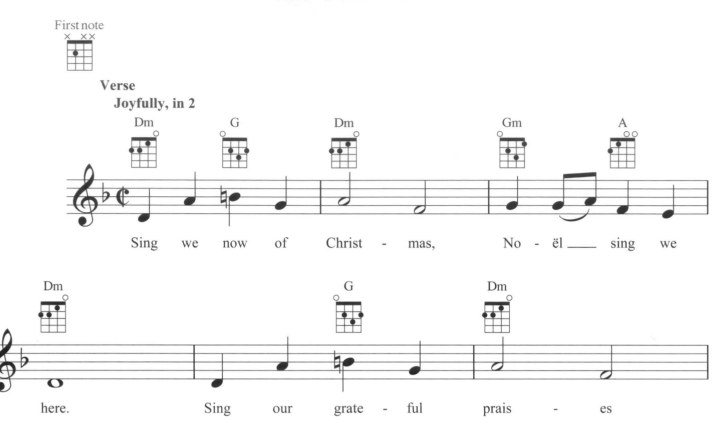

Sing we now of Christ - mas, No - ël ___ sing we

here. Sing our grate - ful prais - es

Chorus

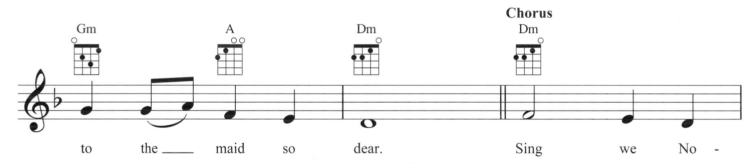

to the ___ maid so dear. Sing we No -

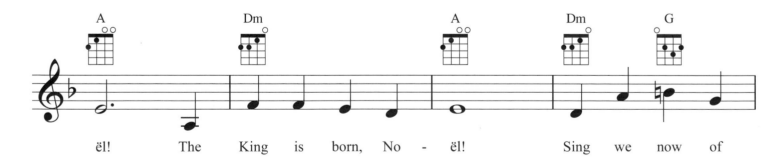

ël! The King is born, No - ël! Sing we now of

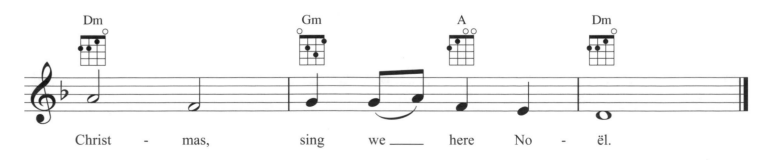

Christ - mas, sing we ___ here No - ël.

Sleep, Holy Babe

Words by Edward Caswell
Music by J.B. Dykes

First note

Verse
Quietly

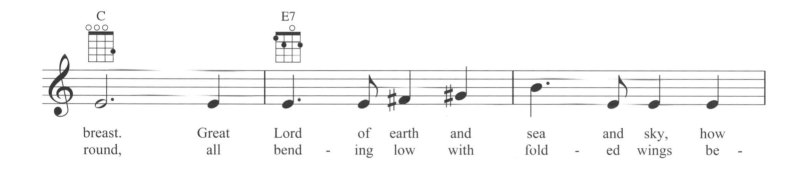

Sleep,   Ho - ly   Babe,   up - on   Thy __ moth - er's
Sleep,   Ho - ly   Babe;   Thine   an - gels __ watch   a -

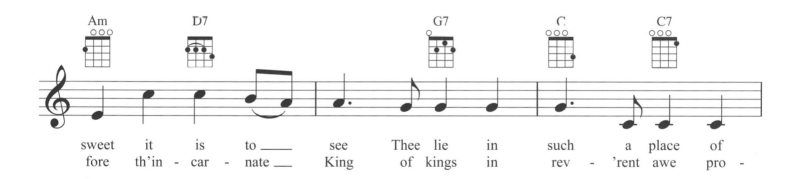

breast.   Great   Lord   of   earth   and   sea   and   sky,   how
round,   all   bend - ing   low   with   fold - ed   wings   be -

sweet   it   is   to ____   see   Thee   lie   in   such   a   place   of
fore   th'in - car - nate ____   King   of   kings   in   rev - 'rent   awe   pro -

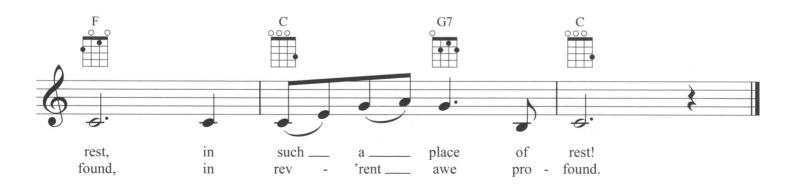

rest,   in   such ____   a ____   place   of   rest!
found,   in   rev - 'rent ____   awe   pro - found.

Sleep, O Sleep, My Lovely Child

Traditional Italian Carol

Still, Still, Still

Salzburg Melody, c.1819
Traditional Austrian Text

1. Still, ___ still, ___ still, to ___ sleep is ___ now His ___ will. On Mar - y's ___ breast He rests in ___ slum - ber, while we ___ pray in end - less ___ num - ber. Still, ___ still, ___ still, to ___ sleep is ___ now His ___ will.

2. Sleep, ___ sleep, ___ sleep, while ___ we Thy ___ vig - il ___ keep. And an - gels ___ come from heav - en ___ sing - ing, songs of ___ ju - bi - la - tion ___ bring - ing. Sleep, ___ sleep, ___ sleep, while ___ we Thy ___ vig - il ___ keep.

Star of the East

Words by George Cooper
Music by Amanda Kennedy

knowing thou beam'st through e - ter - ni - ty.

Help us to fol - low where thou still dost guide

D.C. al Coda

pil grims of earth so wide. _____

Coda

Outro

grave.   O   star   that   leads   to   God ___   a -
o'er   us   leads   still   till   life ___   hath

bove,   whose   rays ___   are   peace, ___   are
ceased.   Beam   on, ___   bright   star, ___   sweet

1.
joy   and ___   love,   watch

2.
Beth - le - hem   star.

There's a Song in the Air

Words and Music by Josiah G. Holland and Karl P. Harrington

1. There's a song in the air! There's a star in the
2. There's a tu - mult of joy o'er the won - der - ful
3. In the light of that star lie the ag - es im -
4. We re - joice in the light, and we ech - o the

sky! There's a moth - er's deep prayer and a ba - by's low
birth, for the vir - gin's sweet boy is the Lord of the
pearled, and that song from a - far has swept o - ver the
song that comes down through the night from the heav - en - ly

cry! And the star rains its fire while the beau - ti - ful
earth. Ay! the star rains its fire while the beau - ti - ful
world. Ev - 'ry hearth is a - flame and the beau - ti - ful
throng. Ay! we shout to the love - ly e - van - gel they

sing, for the man - ger of Beth - le - hem cra - dles a King!
sing, for the man - ger of Beth - le - hem cra - dles a King!
sing in the homes of the na - tions that Je - sus is King!
bring, and we greet in His cra - dle our Sav - ior and King!

Toyland

from BABES IN TOYLAND
Words by Glen MacDonough
Music by Victor Herbert

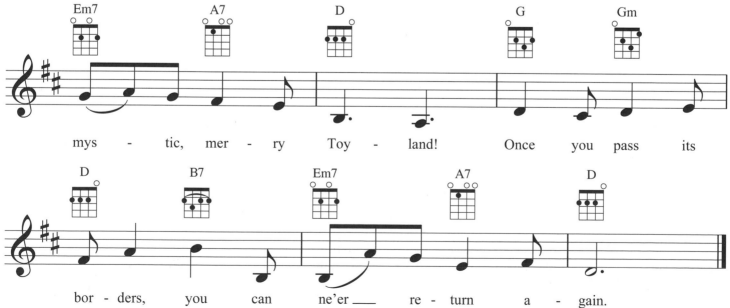

'Twas the Night Before Christmas

Words by Clement Clark Moore
Music by F. Henri Klickman

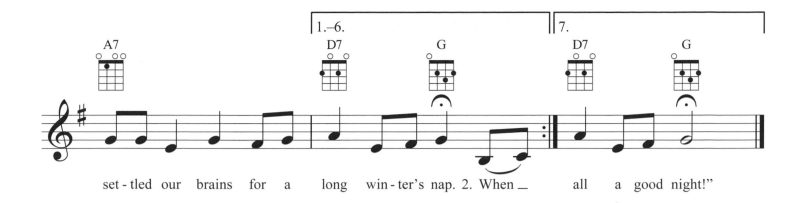

set-tled our brains for a long win-ter's nap. 2. When __ all a good night!"

Additional Lyrics

2. When out on the lawn there arose such a clatter,
   I sprang from my bed to see what was the matter.
   Away to the window I flew like a flash,
   Tore open the shutters and threw up the sash.
   The moon, on the breast of the new-fallen snow,
   Gave a luster of midday to objects below.
   When what to my wondering eyes should appear,
   But a miniature sleigh and eight tiny reindeer.

3. With a little old driver so lively and quick,
   I knew in a moment it must be St. Nick.
   More rapid than eagles his coursers they came,
   And he whistled, and shouted, and called them by name:
   "Now, Dasher! Now, Dancer! Now, Prancer! Now, Vixen!
   On, Comet! On, Cupid! On, Donder and Blitzen!
   To the top of the porch, to the top of the wall!
   Now dash away, dash away, dash away, all!"

4. As dry leaves that before the wild hurricane fly,
   When they meet with an obstacle, mount to the sky,
   So up to the housetop the coursers they flew,
   With the sleigh full of toys and St. Nicholas, too.
   And then in a twinkling I heard on the roof
   The prancing and pawing of each little hoof.
   As I drew in my head and was turning around,
   Down the chimney St. Nicholas came with a bound.

5. He was dressed all in fur from his head to his foot,
   And his clothes were all tarnished with ashes and soot.
   A bundle of toys he had flung on his back,
   And he looked like a peddler just opening his pack.
   His eyes, how they twinkled! His dimples, how merry!
   His cheeks were like roses, his nose like a cherry.
   His droll little mouth was drawn up like a bow,
   And the beard of his chin was as white as the snow.

6. The stump of a pipe he held tight in his teeth,
   And the smoke it encircled his head like a wreath.
   He had a broad face and a round little belly
   That shook when he laughed like a bowl full of jelly.
   He was chubby and plump, a right jolly old elf,
   And I laughed when I saw him, in spite of myself.
   A wink of his eye and a twist of his head
   Soon gave me to know I had nothing to dread.

7. He spoke not a word, but went straight to his work
   And he filled all the stockings, then turned with a jerk.
   And laying a finger aside of his nose,
   And giving a nod, up the chimney he rose.
   He sprang to his sleigh, to his team gave a whistle,
   And away they all flew like the down of a thistle.
   But I heard him exclaim ere he drove out of sight:
   "Happy Christmas to all, and to all a good night!"

The Twelve Days of Christmas

Traditional English Carol

Additional Lyrics

8. On the eighth day... eight maids a-milking...
9. On the ninth day... nine ladies dancing...
10. On the tenth day... ten lords a-leaping...
11. On the 'leventh day... 'leven pipers piping...
12. On the twelfth day... twelve drummers drumming...

A Virgin Unspotted

Traditional English Carol

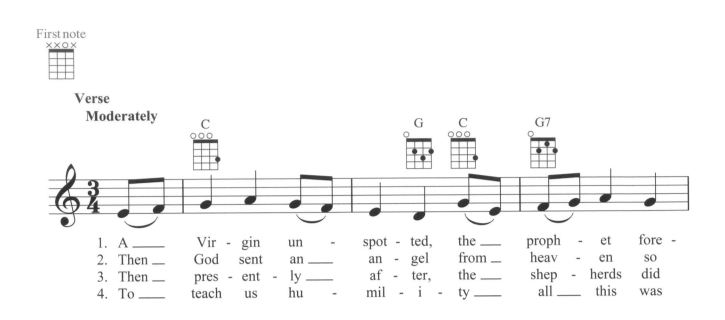

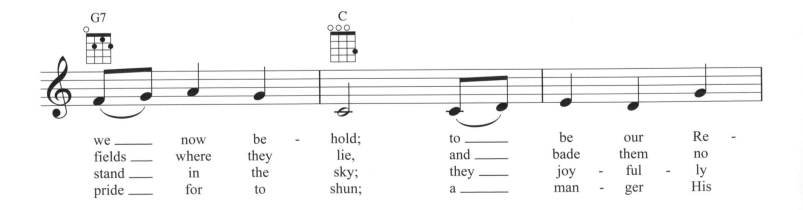

Watchman, Tell Us of the Night

Words by John Bowring
Music by Jacob Hintze

We Wish You a Merry Christmas

Traditional English Folksong

We Three Kings of Orient Are

Words and Music by John H. Hopkins, Jr.

1. We three kings of Or - i - ent are;
2. Born a King on Beth - le - hem plain,
3. Frank - in - cense to of - fer have I;
4., 5. *See additional lyrics*

bear - ing gifts we tra - verse a - far,
gold I bring to crown Him a - gain.
in - cense owns a De - i - ty nigh.

field and foun - tain, moor and moun - tain,
King for - ev - er, ceas - ing nev - er
Pray'r and prais - ing all men rais - ing,

fol - low - ing yon - der star.
o - ver us all to reign.
wor - ship Him, God most high.

Chorus

O _____ star of won - der, star of night,

star with roy - al beau - ty bright,

west - ward lead - ing, still pro - ceed - ing,

guide us to thy per - fect light. light.

Additional Lyrics

4. Myrrh is mine; its bitter perfume
   Breathes a life of gathering gloom;
   Sorr'wing, sighing, bleeding, dying,
   Sealed in the stone-cold tomb.

5. Glorious now, behold Him arise,
   King and God and sacrifice.
   Alleluia, alleluia,
   Sounds through the earth and skies.

Wexford Carol

Traditional Irish Carol

Additional Lyrics

4. With thankful heart and joyful mind,
   The shepherds went the Babe to find,
   And as God's angel had foretold,
   They did our Savior Christ behold.
   Within a manger He was laid,
   And by His side the virgin maid,
   Attending on the Lord of life,
   Who came on earth to end all strife.

5. There were three wise men from afar
   Directed by a glorious star,
   And on they wandered night and day
   Until they came where Jesus lay.
   And when they came unto that place
   Where our beloved Messiah was,
   They humbly cast them at his feet,
   With gifts of gold and incense sweet.

What Child Is This?

Words by William C. Dix
16th Century English Melody

First note

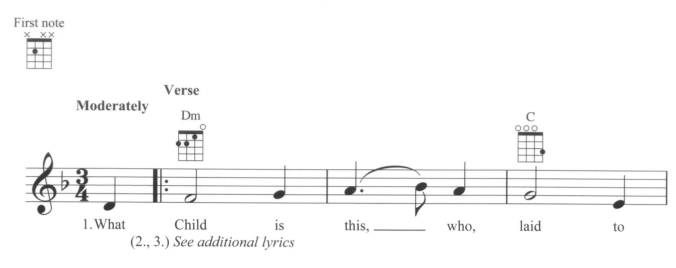

Moderately   **Verse**

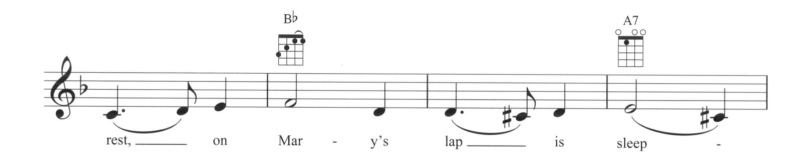

1. What Child is this, _____ who, laid to
(2., 3.) *See additional lyrics*

rest, _____ on Mar - y's lap _____ is sleep -

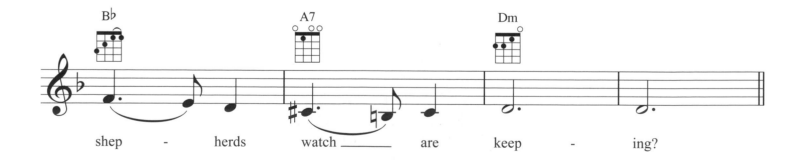

ing; whom an - gels greet _____ with an - thems sweet _____ while

shep - herds watch _____ are keep - ing?

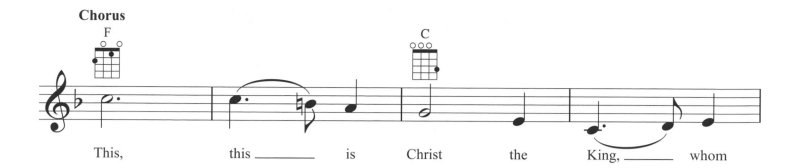

This, this _____ is Christ the King, _____ whom

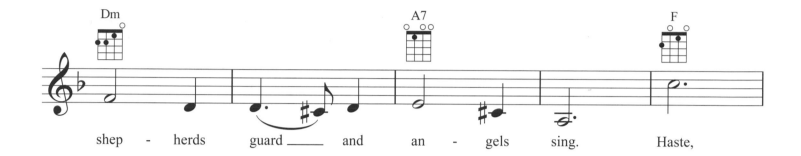

shep - herds guard _____ and an - gels sing. Haste,

haste _____ to bring Him laud, _____ the Babe, _____ the

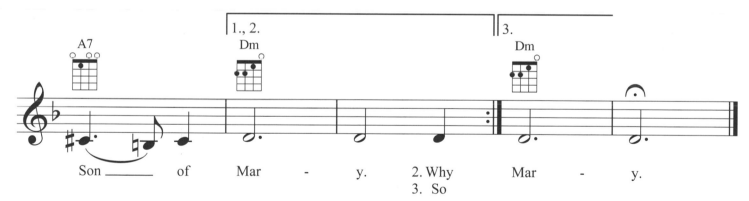

Son _____ of Mar - y. 2. Why Mar - y.
                                          3. So

Additional Lyrics

2. Why lies He in such mean estate
   Where ox and ass are feeding?
   Good Christian, fear, for sinners here
   The silent Word is pleading.

3. So bring Him incense, gold and myrrh.
   Come, peasant, king, to own Him.
   The King of kings salvation brings;
   Let loving hearts enthrone Him.

When Christ Was Born of Mary Free

Music by Arthur H. Brown
Traditional Text, 15th Century

When Christmas Morn Is Dawning

Traditional Swedish

First note

While Shepherds Watched Their Flocks

Words by Nahum Tate
Music by George Frideric Handel

Additional Lyrics

2. "Fear not!" said he, for mighty dread
   Had seized their troubled mind.
   "Glad tidings of great joy I bring
   To you and all mankind,
   To you and all mankind.

3. "To you, in David's town this day,
   Is born of David's line,
   The Savior, who is Christ the Lord;
   And this shall be the sign,
   And this shall be the sign:

4. "The heavenly Babe you there shall find
   To human view displayed,
   All meanly wrapped in swathing bands,
   And in a manger laid,
   And in a manger laid."

5. Thus spake the seraph; and forthwith
   Appeared a shining throng
   Of angels praising God on high,
   Who thus addressed their song,
   Who thus addressed their song:

6. "All glory be to God on high,
   And to the earth be peace;
   Good will henceforth from heav'n to men,
   Begin and never cease,
   Begin and never cease!"

Winds Through the Olive Trees

19th Century American Carol

1. Winds through the ol - ive trees soft - ly did blow
2. Then from the hap - py skies, an - gels bent low,

'round lit - tle Beth - le - hem long, long a - go.
sing - ing their songs of joy long, long a - go.

Sheep on the hill - side lay, whit - er than snow.
For in a man - ger bed, cra - dled we know,

Shep - herds were watch - ing them long, long a - go.
Christ came to Beth - le - hem long, long, a - go.

UKULELE CHORD SONGBOOKS

This series features convenient 6" x 9" books with complete lyrics and chord symbols for dozens of great songs. Each song also includes chord grids at the top of every page and the first notes of the melody for easy reference.

ACOUSTIC ROCK

60 tunes: American Pie • Band on the Run • Catch the Wind • Daydream • Every Rose Has Its Thorn • Hallelujah • Iris • More Than Words • Patience • The Sound of Silence • Space Oddity • Sweet Talkin' Woman • Wake up Little Susie • Who'll Stop the Rain • and more.
00702482 . . . .$15.99

THE BEATLES

100 favorites: Across the Universe • Carry That Weight • Dear Prudence • Good Day Sunshine • Here Comes the Sun • If I Fell • Love Me Do • Michelle • Ob-La-Di, Ob-La-Da • Revolution • Something • Ticket to Ride • We Can Work It Out • and many more.
00703065 . . . .$19.99

BEST SONGS EVER

70 songs: All I Ask of You • Bewitched • Edelweiss • Just the Way You Are • Let It Be • Memory • Moon River • Over the Rainbow • Someone to Watch over Me • Unchained Melody • You Are the Sunshine of My Life • You Raise Me Up • and more.
00117050 . . . .$16.99

CHILDREN'S SONGS

80 classics: Alphabet Song • "C" Is for Cookie • Do-Re-Mi • I'm Popeye the Sailor Man • Mickey Mouse March • Oh! Susanna • Polly Wolly Doodle • Puff the Magic Dragon • The Rainbow Connection • Sing • Three Little Fishies (Itty Bitty Poo) • and many more.
00702473 . . . .$14.99

CHRISTMAS CAROLS

75 favorites: Away in a Manger • Coventry Carol • The First Noel • Good King Wenceslas • Hark! the Herald Angels Sing • I Saw Three Ships • Joy to the World • O Little Town of Bethlehem • Still, Still, Still • Up on the Housetop • What Child Is This? • and more.
00702474 . . . .$14.99

CHRISTMAS SONGS

55 Christmas classics: Do They Know It's Christmas? • Frosty the Snow Man • Happy Xmas (War Is Over) • Jingle-Bell Rock • Little Saint Nick • The Most Wonderful Time of the Year • White Christmas • and more.
00101776 . . . .$14.99

ISLAND SONGS

60 beach party tunes: Blue Hawaii • Day-O (The Banana Boat Song) • Don't Worry, Be Happy • Island Girl • Kokomo • Lovely Hula Girl • Mele Kalikimaka • Red, Red Wine • Surfer Girl • Tiny Bubbles • Ukulele Lady • and many more.
00702471 . . . .$16.99

150 OF THE MOST BEAUTIFUL SONGS EVER

150 melodies: Always • Bewitched • Candle in the Wind • Endless Love • In the Still of the Night • Just the Way You Are • Memory • The Nearness of You • People • The Rainbow Connection • Smile • Unchained Melody • What a Wonderful World • Yesterday • and more.
00117051 . . . .$24.99

PETER, PAUL & MARY

Over 40 songs: And When I Die • Blowin' in the Wind • Goodnight, Irene • If I Had a Hammer (The Hammer Song) • Leaving on a Jet Plane • Puff the Magic Dragon • This Land Is Your Land • We Shall Overcome • Where Have All the Flowers Gone? • and more.
00121822 . . . .$12.99

THREE CHORD SONGS

60 songs: Bad Case of Loving You • Bang a Gong (Get It On) • Blue Suede Shoes • Cecilia • Get Back • Hound Dog • Kiss • Me and Bobby McGee • Not Fade Away • Rock This Town • Sweet Home Chicago • Twist and Shout • You Are My Sunshine • and more.
00702483 . . . .$14.99

TOP HITS

31 hits: The A Team • Born This Way • Forget You • Ho Hey • Jar of Hearts • Little Talks • Need You Now • Rolling in the Deep • Teenage Dream • Titanium • We Are Never Ever Getting Back Together • and more.
00115929 . . . .$14.99

Prices, contents, and availability subject to change without notice.

www.halleonard.com